HOMELAND SECURITY AT THE STATE LEVEL

HOMELAND
SECURITY
AT THE
STATE LEVEL

A Primer on State Homeland Security Programs

DICK CAÑAS

FOREWORD
by
Dennis R. Schrader,
former Maryland Homeland Security Advisor

authorHOUSE®

AuthorHouse™
1663 Liberty Drive
Bloomington, IN 47403
www.authorhouse.com
Phone: 1-800-839-8640

Published by AuthorHouse   08/14/2012

ISBN: 978-1-4772-6082-1 (sc)
ISBN: 978-1-4772-6081-4 (e)

Library of Congress Control Number: 2012914821

Table of Contents

Chapters

Foreword

I first met Dick Cañas in early 2006 soon after he was appointed as the first Homeland Security Advisor to New Jersey Governor Jon S. Corzine. Tom Moran and I visited with Dick to brief him about the All Hazards Consortium and the collaboration of the Mid-Atlantic states. As Executive Director of the Consortium, Tom Moran tenaciously ensured that the regional leaders were connected.

Dick embraced the Consortium and became a regional leader along with Bob Crouch from Virginia as I was leaving the Maryland Governor's office in 2007. Tom Moran first recognized in 2007 that the state and local governments would experience routine and significant leadership turnover that caused states face the challenge of bridging the learning curve. This is not unusual and states confront these issues routinely for subjects like education, public safety, and health.

However, Homeland Security is an evolving field that has put the state and local governments and the private sector of our nation as integral pieces of the domestic component of our national security architecture. Regional collaboration has been one of the national priorities since National Preparedness Goal was first envisioned and the Target capabilities were established.

The challenge for state, local, governments, and the private sector is that we are still in the first generation of homeland security professionals. These professionals have been developing the discipline in this past decade since 9/11. Over the next decade it will be important to capture and preserve the precepts of the discipline and shorten the cycle time to develop new leaders.

The other challenge is that most strategy, doctrine, and tools that have been developed have been federal centric and not reflective of the challenges faced by state, local, and private interests. The National

Governor's Association has a very nice Guide for Governors and established a best practices center for homeland security.

When new state and local administrations begin their initial transition, there will be new senior leaders who will normally have special knowledge in government or the private sector or may even have knowledge and experience in an element of homeland security like intelligence, law enforcement, or health care. The challenge is to quickly climb the learning curve that is the homeland security enterprise.

The handbook covers several topics that provide a state level flavor to discipline. For example, Chapter 12 on legal issues is a very important chapter. Every state has a different approach. When I was in Maryland we adopted the Anti-Terrorism Advisory Council model (ATAC) established by the Department of Justice. The ATAC was chaired by the Assistant U.S. Attorney. This proved very helpful since there needed to be a legal foundation and oversight for the fusion center that protected civil liberties.

The other practical issue is how to build a state, local, or private sector program that will sustain itself through the resource constraints that will occur as the public loses interest in the security subject. It is imperative to build programs that leverage collaborative resources and avoid creating expensive capabilities that won't survive without federal money.

For example, we actually put our fusion center in the FBI in anticipation that fusion centers would be difficult to sustain in the long run.

It is a privilege to collaborate with Dick Cañas on this handbook.

Dennis R. Schrader, June 1, 2010

Preface

The primary intent of this booklet is to break down in simple terms the various parts that make up *state* homeland security, as opposed to the national effort led by the U. S. Department of Homeland Security (DHS). We discuss examples of strategies, plans and processes used by state homeland security advisors in their individual efforts to prevent and prepare for both man-made *and* natural disasters. Since states vary in their approaches, we have kept discussions in general terms.

Much has been written about the subject, quite comprehensively and in technical terms. The McGraw-Hill Homeland Security Handbook: The Definitive Guide for Law Enforcement, Emergency Management Technicians (EMT), and All Other Security Professionals,[1] is an example.

In contrast, this booklet is directed at a more general audience not necessarily the homeland security professional. A simple Question & Answer format is used to supplement understanding of concepts and terminologies and to answer rudimentary questions as might be posed by an interested, yet casually informed, public.

Basic questions about:

- ✓ The Role of DHS
- ✓ Information sharing programs
- ✓ Risk-based management
- ✓ Public/private partnerships
- ✓ Fusion centers
- ✓ Emergency operating centers
- ✓ The Federal Emergency Management Agency (FEMA)

---

[1] The McGraw-Hill Homeland Security Handbook, David Kamien, 2006, The McGraw-Hill Company, Inc.

- ✓ Critical infrastructure and key resources
- ✓ Grant programs
- ✓ Preparedness and prevention programs
- ✓ Public Awareness
- ✓ Legal issues.

The content also focuses on the relationships required of a comprehensive state homeland security program—a relationship that encompasses state and local (S/L) governments, the private sector, and the public at large.

Because *federal* homeland security initiatives get mixed into the overall *state* prevention and preparedness efforts, we attempt to point out, in lay person terms, some of the more important differences and intersections between state and federal efforts.

The main focus, however, is promoting an understanding of state characteristics when it comes to homeland security. For example, S/L emergency agencies are budgeted to focus on "all-crimes/all-hazards/all-the-time." That means that local emergencies (accidents, crime suppression, firefighting, medical emergencies, school security, to name the more prevalent) will always take precedence over national planning for possible catastrophic disasters. Furthermore, S/L emergency response is decentralized and autonomous. That means that incorporated towns, cities, counties, territories and tribal nations have individual governments and emergency agencies that, for the most part, are independent of each other.

Understanding state processes is the first step towards collaboration, and this booklet strives to provide that understanding and promote uniformity.

As backdrop and reference, we devote the opening chapter to a cursory description of the U. S. Department of Homeland Security's missions, as well as the missions of DHS's various federal components.

But, the focus of this primer is the complex environment of *state* homeland security.

Introduction

Eleven years have passed since the tragic events of 9/11 and we continue to struggle with what is meant by the term "homeland security," or as some locals call it, "home*town* security." The term refers to the protection, i.e., safety and security, of people, properties and interests within the borders of the United States of America.

And that is simple enough.

But we also hear people refer to "*national* security" and "homeland *defense*" as though they were synonymous with "homeland security." They are not.

What's the difference?

The simple explanation is that "national security" includes the protection of our people, properties and interests from enemies staging or emanating hostile activities from <u>outside</u> U.S. borders. Homeland security is domestically focused, i.e., protecting the homeland from both man-made and natural disasters. These disasters include accidents, pandemics, hurricanes and terrorist acts.

Observers are often confused by the inevitable overlap in foreign and domestic security efforts. For example, the terms Weapons of Mass Destruction (WMDs) and Improvised Explosive Devices (IEDs) are terms used in discussing both foreign and domestic threats. Terrorists themselves come in different forms, the "home-grown" variety, e.g., Timothy McVeigh, and foreign-based factions such as Al Qaeda. Unfortunately, the term "war on terrorism" does not alleviate confusion even for the federal government. The debate over prosecuting terrorists in "war tribunals" versus the U.S. criminal justice system is just one illustration of this on-going confusion.

So, is it as simple as: Terrorism abroad is the responsibility of one set of defenders (warriors), but at home (the continental United States) it is the domain of law enforcement and the legal system?

In its simplest form, yes, but there other considerations. The U.S. legal system and homeland security can reach beyond our borders through extraditions treaties and bilateral and multilateral agreements for example, but most security activities are focused domestically. Our national security and our homeland security are the responsibility of the President. Abroad, the Department of Defense, the Department of State, and the Intelligence community (IC) primarily lead national security—a *completely federal response*. The U. S. Department of Homeland Security (DHS), established in 2003, is also a member of the Executive Branch along with the Department of Justice and their sub-agencies, and it leads the *federal* response to domestic security and disaster events.

So far, so good.

Confusion often lies in the fact that security at home *is not exclusively a federal effort*. The job of protecting citizens, critical infrastructure and interests at home against all day-to-day crimes and hazards falls primarily on the shoulders of independent state, county, municipal, tribal and private agencies, each with different authorities and jurisdictions down to their meager budgets. *This fact is the 800 pound gorilla in the room*, and the reason why information-sharing and intercommunication strategies are often gridlocked eleven years after 9/11. The most recent examples of jurisdictional confusion are the 2009 Christmas Day bomber, Fort Hood shooting and the 2012 Sikh Temple shooting. When the information points to "domestic Terrorism," the FBI will take the investigative lead. Often critical information is in the possession of the emergency responders and the S/L authorities, in which case coordination between them is critical.

How diverse and disproportionate are these domestic agencies?

Just take critical infrastructure for example: 85% of the sectors essential to maintaining life (i.e., water, food, shelter, energy, health care), are the responsibility of private sector or non-governmental organizations (NGOs). And look at domestic law enforcement activity: just 60 major cities police departments, all independent of each other, account for 80% of arrests and crime statistics in the country. Then, consider the 50 states (not counting territories), 3,444 counties, 150 major cities (not counting municipalities under a million in population), and dozens of tribal nations, each possessing security agencies with different levels of authority, each acting independent of one another.

Would it be more effective if we consolidated efforts as in other countries?

Well, yes, but there is a major principle at play. This "home-rule" configuration actually defines this country and who we are as Americans. This principle happens to be protected by the 23rd Amendment of the Constitution of the United States. And, since all emergencies start with a robust local government response, there is a strong argument that in this large diverse country having well training and equipped local responders is more efficient.

The U.S. Constitution, you say?

Our forefathers listed our inalienable rights within the Constitution as a series of mandates protecting our civil and state's rights. These sacred freedoms cannot be ignored by unbridled or unlimited security measures nor can they be superseded by any federal authority other than by Constitutional amendment. In other words, DON'T MESS WITH THEM unless it is a life or death situation, and then it better be a catastrophe, and you still better get a judicial ruling, if at all feasible!

And who, pray tell, is charged with maintaining the balance between protecting these liberties and the public's safety?

Ultimately, the Supreme Court, but in 99.9999% of cases, it is an army of lawyers. We are a nation of laws, with no more tortuous a process within the bureaucracy than legal and tort review of decisions. Viewed through this prism, coordinating a domestic prevention and protection strategy for U. S. people, properties and interests is a dynamic and formidable challenge. It is the main reason we continue debating and adjusting many recommendations of the 9/11 Commission. The bad news is that the challenges are formidable; the good news is that those charged with public safety are relentlessly and constantly addressing the demands.

But why do you need rudimentary knowledge about homeland security?

It is our contention that "homeland security" must be all-inclusive, that is, prevention and preparedness involves everyone: public sector, private sector, and the citizenry. Plus, it's going to be around for a long time. People continue to be drawn into the effort at all levels. Solutions have to be *regional*, *inclusive*, and *transparent*.

It should be pointed out that the concept of homeland security is not new. The Hart-Rudman Task Force on Homeland Security (officially known as the U.S. Commission on National Security/21st Century [USCNS/21])[2] was chartered in 1998. At the time, it was the most comprehensive review on national security since the National Security Act of 1947. Among other things, USCNS/21 spoke to homeland vulnerabilities and the blurring of boundaries between homeland defense and foreign policies. In many ways, the establishment of DHS built on several of the recommendations of USCNS/21.

But let's face it, since 9/11 the term "homeland security" has permeated the jargon of the media and the public. Private and governmental agencies have instituted homeland security offices, departments, divisions, sections, programs, liaisons, or points of contact. Government regulations were not far behind requiring public and private enterprises to include security/disaster planning as part of their operational plans.

Rudimentary understanding of homeland security is a must, even for the average person.

---

[2]   USCNS/21, *New World Coming: American Security in the 21st Century* (Washington, DC: US Government Printing Office, September 1999), v.

Why does one get the impression that interest in homeland security has diminished?

As we distance ourselves from the shock and outrage of 9/11 and the dismal government response to Hurricane Katrina, interest in homeland security issues has waned. But in 2009, a series of terrorist incidents tied to Al Qaeda and affiliates have reinvigorated public concern. An angry President re-prioritized counterterrorism efforts after the Christmas Day bombing attempt on a U.S. airliner, highlighting the level of complacency over the past few years. Terrorism with a foreign nexus has increased this past year and threats are expected to continue into the foreseeable future. Unfortunately, there are still numbers of psychopaths walking around undetected at home. They pop up their ugly heads periodically as hate criminals or "lone wolves" that need public engagement to subsidize their policing, whether it's a Colorado movie house or Wisconsin Sikh Temple.

And let's not forget the need for preparedness against natural disasters. The only thing predictable about Mother Nature is that she is unpredictable, and most importantly—deadly unpredictable. The hundreds of thousands killed in Haiti's earthquake in 2010 will remain a somber reminder for quite some time. Google global or natural disasters sometime and note their degree of frequency.

For the foreseeable future, homeland security will remain a priority, especially during stressful economic times and international terrorist organizations continue to plot to do us harm at home. We cannot be lulled into complacency because Osama Bin Laden and Al Qaeda leadership have been killed.

Federal funding (otherwise known as the "dash-for-the-cash" by government contractors) remains a good employment opportunity. Each year, federal funding for homeland security continues to rise despite a challenged economy. How the Washington-led policies and procedures trickle down to state, local, and tribal planners, responders, managers, assessors and mediators, i.e., how they are implemented and how effective they are, remain key questions, and the subject of ongoing studies and adjustments. Keep in mind that although this threat is national in scope and requires federal attention and funding, all emergencies start locally and remain so with injuries and loss of services felt immediately at the local level by you, us, and our families. It will be some time, unfortunately, before the information contained in this book is irrelevant.

So, what are the basic facts one can take away from this book?

A number of things.

First, <u>every state has a homeland security office, independent of federal DHS</u>, run by homeland security advisers reporting directly or indirectly to their respective governors. I know you'll be shocked to hear that these 50 homeland security offices are not organized similarly (*naturally*, given the 23rd Amendment). Within most states, independent county and municipal governments have their own "emergency management office" (*naturally*, given our proclivity to home-rule). And, within the counties, municipalities and tribal groups, there are innate "cultural" differences within the various agencies (*naturally*, lest you think firefighters, police officers, and medical responders all drink the same Kool-aide). This book attempts to describe the basic interaction and processes in this context.

Secondly, <u>emergency response and counterterrorism at the state, local, and tribal level are administered under an all-crimes/all-hazards paradigm</u>, i.e, all crimes and emergencies are local, or at least that is how they all start. These threats vary in size and by region, but there are commonalities. There are tried and true lessons-learned from individual programs among the various state homeland security offices. For example, most governors consider school and campus security to be a homeland security matter when incidents are beyond the capabilities of departments of education and higher education to handle. U. S. DHS does *not*.

This book breaks down and defines in lay-person's terms the most common terms and components of homeland security concepts such as regionalization, inter-dependencies, resiliency, and interoperability.

And lastly, this thought: Perhaps, one day there won't be enemies of the state desperately trying through violent means to change our way of life, and perhaps Mother Nature will be more predictable and less deadly. Until then, however, it is incumbent on all of us to be conversant, if even at the most rudimentary levels regarding terms, strategies, processes, goals and objectives of the homeland security efforts within our respective regions. It was with this intent and purpose that this handbook was assembled.

Chapter 1

The U.S. Department of Homeland Security (The Feds)

It is safe to say that it was the harrowing events of September 11, 2001 that led to establishing the U. S. Department of Homeland Security (DHS) in 2003. This act of Congress followed a series of national-level policies and new authorities enacted by Congress. DHS' origins are directly linked to the ongoing processes of preventing acts of terrorism against the homeland. Following Hurricane Katrina in 2005, DHS expanded its preparedness mission even further and directed the Federal Emergency Management Agency (FEMA) to more vigorously and effectively respond to natural disasters.

DHS is a Cabinet-level Department in the US Government. Its authority and responsibility are to prevent and prepare for disasters and oversee the security and safety of the homeland. Major federal agencies, especially those overseeing our borders, transportation, and disaster response were brought under one roof. Currently, there are 16 major parts to DHS according to their website, *www.dhs.gov*.

The Directorate for National Protection and Programs works to advance the Department's risk-reduction mission. Reducing risk requires an integrated approach that encompasses both physical and virtual threats and their associated human elements.

The Directorate for Science and Technology is the primary research and development arm of the Department. It provides federal, state and local officials with the technology and capabilities to protect the homeland.

1

The <u>Directorate for Management</u> is responsible for Department budgets and appropriations, expenditure of funds, accounting and finance, procurement; human resources, information technology systems, facilities and equipment, and the identification and tracking of performance measurements.

The <u>Office of Policy</u> is the primary policy formulation and coordination component for the Department of Homeland Security. It provides a centralized, coordinated focus to the development of Department-wide, long-range planning to protect the United States.

The <u>Office of Health Affairs</u> coordinates all medical activities of the Department of Homeland Security to ensure appropriate preparation for and response to incidents having medical significance.

The <u>Office of Intelligence and Analysis</u> is responsible for using information and intelligence from multiple sources to identify and assess current and future threats to the United States.

The <u>Office of Operations Coordination</u> is responsible for monitoring the security of the United States on a daily basis and coordinating activities within the Department and with governors, Homeland Security Advisers, law enforcement partners, and critical infrastructure operators in all 50 states and more than 50 major urban areas nationwide.

The <u>Federal Law Enforcement Training Center</u> provides career-long training to law enforcement professionals to help them fulfill their responsibilities safely and proficiently.

The <u>Domestic Nuclear Detection Office</u> works to enhance the nuclear detection efforts of federal, state, territorial, tribal, and local governments, and the private sector and to ensure a coordinated response to such threats.

<u>The Transportation Security Administration</u> (TSA) protects the nation's transportation systems to ensure freedom of movement for people and commerce.

<u>States Border Protection Agency</u> is responsible for protecting our nation's borders in order to prevent terrorists and terrorist weapons from entering the United States, while facilitating the flow of legitimate trade and travel.

<u>United States Citizenship and Immigration Services</u> is responsible for the administration of immigration and naturalization adjudication functions and establishing immigration services policies and priorities.

<u>United States Immigration and Customs Enforcement</u> (ICE), the largest investigative arm of the Department of Homeland Security, is responsible for identifying and shutting down vulnerabilities in the nation's border, economic, transportation and infrastructure security.

<u>The United States Coast Guard</u> protects the public, the environment, and U.S. economic interests—in the nation's ports and waterways, along the coast, on international waters, or in any maritime region as required to support national security.

<u>The Federal Emergency Management Agency</u> (FEMA) prepares the nation for hazards, manages Federal response and recovery efforts following any national incident, and administers the National Flood Insurance Program.

<u>The United States Secret Service</u> protects the President and other high-level officials and investigates counterfeiting and other financial crimes, including financial institution fraud, identity theft, computer fraud; and computer-based attacks on our nation's financial, banking, and telecommunications infrastructure.

Each part is separated into four main functions:

- ✓ Counterterrorism
- ✓ Border Security
- ✓ Preparedness, Response, Recovery
- ✓ Immigration

In February of 2010, DHS issued its first Quadrennial Homeland Security Review Report: A Strategic Framework for a Secure Homeland.[3].

As outlined in the report, there are five DHS missions:

Mission 1: Preventing Terrorism and Enhancing Security

- Goal 1.1: Prevent terrorist attacks
- Goal 1.2: Prevent the unauthorized acquisition or use of chemical, biological, radiological, and nuclear materials and capabilities
- Goal 1.3: Manage risks to critical infrastructure, key leadership, and events

Mission 2: Securing and Managing Our Borders

- Goal 2.1: Effectively control U.S. air, land, and sea borders
- Goal 2.2: Safeguard lawful trade and travel
- Goal 2.3: Disrupt and dismantle transnational criminal organizations

Mission 3: Enforcing and Administering Our Immigration Laws

- Goal 3.1: Strengthen and effectively administer the immigration system
- Goal 3.2: Prevent unlawful immigration

Mission 4: Safeguarding and Securing Cyberspace

- Goal 4.1: Create a safe, secure, and resilient cyber environment
- Goal 4.2: Promote cyber-security knowledge and innovation

---

[3] Quadrennial Homeland Security Review Report: A Strategic Framework for a Secure Homeland, February 2010, Department of Homeland Security printing. Also, see www.dhs.gov.

Mission 5: Ensuring Resilience to Disasters

• Goal 5.1: Mitigate hazards
• Goal 5.2: Enhance preparedness
• Goal 5.3: Ensure effective emergency response
• Goal 5.4: Rapidly recover

Do the states use the same model, i.e., mission goals, for their programs?

Not entirely. States that have land border crossings are engaged with federal border security agencies and immigration. States that have major airports and critical infrastructure also work closely with federal counterparts, such as TSA. But the states themselves do not have immigration or customs regulating agencies, despite efforts to change this constitutional law by some states. States do tend to use similar models when it comes to disaster preparedness, intelligence sharing, and resiliency programs. As we will discuss later, state priorities differ mainly in what is perceived as security threats. For example, drugs, gangs and violence are the main preoccupation of local law enforcement in populous urban areas. Locals have to live with the fact that a major disaster or international threat will surely overwhelm their response capabilities.

So, if a disaster strikes the U.S., DHS is in charge of the response?

Well, that all depends on the size and type of disaster. Each emergency starts out with a local response. The World Trade Center attack on 9/11 is a case in point. It was local police, firefighters and emergency medical services that were the first responders.

The rule of thumb is that if the disaster at home is major or "mega" in size (e.g., hurricane, pandemic, international terrorism, or overwhelms the state's capabilities), DHS will lead the federal support and response. DHS' mission is to support the local response, but let's be honest, if a nuclear attack occurs on U.S. soil, the federal government is *not* going to wait for a governor to ask for help. It is our measured conclusion that the event will be treated as a national security breach, and any survivors and aftermath can expect to fall under a federal authority—and so it should be. However, do not expect things to initially run smoothly. The local situation will require immediate decisions and, at the moment of the event, planning is impossible.

Since Hurricane Katrina, DHS has erred on the side of caution and pre-positioned staff, especially from the Federal Emergency Management Agency (FEMA), at the state level in anticipation of an emergency that may meet the federal assistance threshold. An example of this is regional and local flooding. FEMA is usually on the scene before a state emergency is declared. That policy is a positive reaction to the lessons-learned following Katrina.

What does the phrase "command and control" mean during emergencies?

Basically, it means: Who is in charge? And, what protocols are being used to manage the emergency? Most states follow the federal guidelines of the National Incident Management System (NIMS)[4], which was established to standardize components, concepts and principles of emergency response, no matter the size or nature of the emergency. Through NIMS, states strive to follow a common incident command system (ICS). A check of the individual state emergency management offices' websites can provide local ICS protocols for managing personnel, communications, facilities, and resources. In emergency management, establishing "command and control" is one of the most, if not the most, critical parts of response.

But, if it's an act of terrorism, the Feds are definitely in charge of the investigation, Right?

For the most part, that is correct. First responders will undoubtedly be state and locals (S/L), but the second wave will be federal agencies, and remember, often that will take time. But keep in mind that when discussing terrorism investigations, the Feds are not DHS, but the Federal Bureau of Investigation (FBI), which is part of the Justice Department.

---

[4] Homeland Security Presidential Directive #5 (HSPD-5), President George W. Bush, E.O. 26, 1996, and updated 2006 as Executive Order 26.1

Most states (if not all) have state statutes that cover acts of terrorism, but by agreements between the FBI field offices and states' Attorneys General, the FBI has right of first refusal on terrorism investigations. Thankfully, this is no longer a jurisdictional "turf" issue.

How so?

Two major changes occurred within the FBI to manage such disputes. First, the FBI created Joint Terrorism Task Forces (JTTF) in all of their 90-plus field offices and these JTTFs specialize in counterterrorism and freely invite S/L police agencies to participate as <u>full partners</u> under FBI supervision. (This is not your father's FBI.) As a result of the Bureau's inclusiveness policies, they benefit from additional resources and local expertise and the S/Ls stay informed—a win-win for all. And second, the feds have more resources and funding to handle long-term complicated investigations that may require months or even years of surveillance and monitoring of suspects. A local police department does not have this type of staying power. We'll cover this subject in more detail in Chapter 6.

Then, how does DHS administer its mission to prevent terrorism?

Keep in mind that the FBI's main focus is to investigate federal crimes, and terrorism is one. They do some outreach and have pro-active community programs on crime suppression, but that is not their primary mission. However, one of DHS' primary missions is preventing acts of terrorism at home—a daunting challenge. Besides organizing systematic outreach to avert, say, the radicalization of young people, DHS has a critical role in developing a system to share credible and relevant information with the public, as well as between the federal Intelligence community (IC) and S/L agencies.

Admittedly, DHS' role as the conduit for information on federal counterterrorism activities to the public and S/L agencies *during* an act of terrorism is hampered by legal constraints. Classified information and rules of criminal procedures about public or unauthorized disclosure usually apply. Comparatively speaking, the media has the advantage on providing "latest news" because they are not a government agency representing "the people," and they have lesser requirements to confirm the accuracy of information. To the extent possible, DHS is attempting to bridge this information gap with S/Ls where possible.

What exactly are they doing to fix this problem?

When it comes to information sharing on terrorism, DHS is both the problem and the solution. The need to share timely, valuable and credible information on terrorism threats and attacks with the public and local authorities is often handcuffed by national security restrictions placed on them by the Justice Department and the IC. Many times this is due to the sensitivity of ongoing investigations. The main deficiencies in information sharing are the lack of timeliness and an effective means to deliver it. There are over 100,000 independent law enforcement agencies in this country not counting private-sector security forces, and most officials do not have security clearances. That said, DHS is the only federal department that has the authority and responsibility to develop a solution to effective information sharing, which was the number one recommendation of the *9/11 Commission Report*.[5]

DHS is addressing relations with S/Ls and the private sector by dispersing resident DHS representatives around the country and supporting the development of regional S/L intelligence centers (see Chapter 6). At last count, there were over 60 of these "fusion" centers. DHS is also including S/Ls in ad hoc task forces and working groups to develop solutions for complex national problems such as information sharing and radicalization. But when it comes to ongoing terrorist activities in the homeland, the rules of criminal procedures and the compartmentalization of sensitive information require DHS to constantly update their liaison and partnership efforts.

Is DHS too big?

Some think so. There are compelling arguments by experts to suggest that, yes, it has too many moving parts. DHS has over 300,000

---

[5]   The National Commission on Terrorist Attacks Upon the United States, aka, The 9/11 Commission Report, May 27, 2004

employees and five principal missions. Most security agencies have only one overarching mission usually described in a word or sentence, such as fire suppression, law and order, planning and prevention, intelligence, neutralize the enemy, etc.

Consider DHS's span: It is responsible for protecting the president and family (past and present), guarding the borders (on land and sea), securing the safety of the traveling public (air, land, and sea), immigration (all points of entry), customs enforcement and regulations, federal emergency management, protecting critical infrastructure and key resources (see Chapter 8), and other management and administrative responsibilities. On first blush, the idea that one department can give priority attention to each does not seem plausible. But, before jumping on the criticism bandwagon, you should also consider that preventing, preparing and reacting to a major disaster (remember, we are still reeling from the experiences of 9/11 and Katrina) requires the integration of all of these security and safety functions, including executive protection and immigration. And Washington does love "one-stop-shopping."

There is an accepted premise in Washington that it takes about eight years for a new federal department to be established efficiently and to be accepted as a federal staple (Defense took decades). In that regard, DHS continues "dance as fast as it can." Given that rule of thumb, it may be time now to revisit the question.

What is the greatest challenge facing DHS in the immediate future?

Funny you should ask. This question is a great bridge to the following chapters, beginning with "Interagency Coordination." The truth is that DHS is caught in a schizophrenic challenge when it comes to information sharing. It needs to be part of the federal Intelligence community *and* bridge the sharing of classified information with S/Ls, but it also wants to lead an effort to make better use of "raw" S/L information. The first goal is restrained because IC information is usually classified and can't be shared systematically with S/Ls. The second goal is challenged by decentralized S/L record management systems (RMSs).

"Decentralized" record management systems?

DHS correctly asserts that the "eyes 'n ears" of S/Ls and the private-sector are critical, if not mandatory, to detecting terrorists plotting an attack on the homeland. However, the lack of centralized records or the resources to analyze unfiltered data are the "long poles in the tent." DHS is not "tooled" to do this either. To convince S/Ls to reorganize their operational information and provide it to DHS, in order to "connect-the-dots" requires a comprehensive implementation plan and funding. The plan must recognize that RMSs are set up in an all-crimes paradigm, which is the domain of S/L law enforcement.

The IC is organized and generously funded to perform collection and analysis *internationally* for national security purposes. Meanwhile, there is no public or political will to authorize DHS or any other federal department to form a "domestic CIA." That may be the greatest challenge facing DHS today, namely, harnessing the power of the information contained in the hundreds of thousands of unclassified, un-vetted and un-centralized record management systems, which contain the "dots," *and then*, connecting them.

The first step towards such a solution is for DHS to clearly understand individual state homeland security operations.

Chapter 2

Interagency Coordination

There is a Mexican saying, "*Hablando se entiende la gente.*" Roughly translated, it means: "Dialogue leads to understanding." Every profession, trade, discipline, sport, and similar grouping tends to have its own "culture," slang, accepted practices, tolerance, and defense mechanisms. My favorite bumper sticker at a firefighter's convention was: "*If you can't stand the heat, become a cop.*" So, it stands to reason that when you pull together a group of people with different backgrounds and missions, to establish, say an interagency task force or working group, the chair better have the wisdom of Solomon and the patience of Job.

As homeland security experts, Eric and Jeff Kutner, of the Emergency Response Design Group opine: *solving communications and information technology interoperability gets much of the attention; what is ignored is "human interoperability"—many people just don't want to communicate or work together.*

In the business of Homeland Security, the interagency process is unavoidable and indispensable.

Why unavoidable and indispensable?

The nature of emergencies combines a unique set of critical but unanticipated circumstances and people with diverse backgrounds and interests. Prevention and preparedness efforts must include all these people. In homeland security, the emergency response community (ERC) consists of, at the very least, police, fire, medical and HazMat specialists (think 9-1-1 phone calls). In larger emergencies, you can add to that group: utility companies, mass transit agencies, non-governmental agencies such as the Red Cross, select private sectors, elected representatives, etc. And that list doesn't include federal partners. Thus, you have an idea of the variety of "cultures" that have to understand, agree, and relate to a chosen course(s) of action or strategy.

The reason they call it, "crisis management," is because during a crisis, the consequences of inaction or autonomous, uncoordinated action(s) are dire. Managing an inclusive, and transparent relationship in the ERC is the goal of an effective state Homeland Security program. Issues simply need to be adequately vetted.

What's "vetted?"

Vetting is a Washington bureaucratic term. Its more commonly used as "to pass muster" or gain approval by stakeholders. What it really means is that *all* the interested parties are given an opportunity to voice their opinion on an issue being debated. Managing the vetting process is an art form and, if done properly, maximizes a unified position. Opinions and counter-opinions also have to be shared. The trick is to control the vetting process so you do not end up with what you often see today in Congress—seemingly endless point and counterpoint by interest groups on contentious issues—gridlock. Preparedness for emergencies demands a unified position, or as the military describes it, a force-multiplier.

What are the basic rules you have to keep in mind to run an effective interagency group?

Inclusiveness is one. While it might sound counter-intuitive, the more people involved in emergency preparedness the better. Responding to emergencies is another matter, but that is where protocols come in.

At the state level, homeland security falls under the governor. He or she has to set the priority and leadership for prevention and preparedness. Most discussions and liaison involving homeland security should be led by the governor or his/her representative, usually the state's Homeland Security Advisor (HSA).

Inclusiveness starts when preparing the list of invitees to an interagency preparedness meeting. It is usually the representative who you fail to include who cause the most friction afterward. Another advantage of having the governor or HSA chair the meeting is that no one will quarrel with the choice. The same logic applies if the emergency is confined to a locality, e.g., an incorporated municipality, territory, or county. The recognized authority or their representative has to set the policy of inclusiveness.

Institutionalizing preparedness and planning stages in the process is another basic tenet for successful interagency coordination. It is true that a main characteristic of an emergency is crisis management. During an accident or terrorist event, for example, it is the first responders, the ERC, who are pressure-tested. When there is time to plan, however, as in anticipation of a hurricane or pandemic, the planners may or may not have ERC experience. One way to avert such leadership gaps is having the ERC actively participate in the planning and exercising stages.

What does "planning and exercising stages" mean?

Staging exercises, whether "table-top" (discussion and role-playing about a hypothetical event "around a meeting table") or practical field exercises away from the office (more effective), is one way of flushing issues about command and control, procedures and protocols.

ERC members taking the time to visit one-on-one with other key players and executives under non-emergency circumstances is another. After all, the first time you meet someone from the ERC should not be *during an emergency.* Visiting agencies during their "monthly" operations meetings is another way of engaging each other before the fact. For example, in New Jersey, every superintendent of school, every college/ university president, every county prosecutor, major chiefs of police, state fire and police organizations, and so forth, have monthly meeting. I am sure other jurisdictions are the same. As an ERC member, getting on their agenda to describe your respective mission is not difficult, in fact, it is welcomed. And, it will pay off dividends later.

No one can predict where the next active shooter or terrorist event will take place. Just keep reminding the pros that if it happens in their area, they had better be prepared. Works great. If not, you have reason to want answers.

What makes an interagency meeting effective? Necessary?

Meetings . . . meetings . . . meetings . . . Unfortunately, you can't avoid meetings when vetting homeland security issues—too many moving parts. (Only bureaucratic government officials and professors love meetings.) You first have to recognize that too many of them are a waste of time. Have you ever attended a meeting that lasted hours and left you dizzy?

So, the first rule is: <u>Don't waste people's time</u>. Meetings should be short (less than an hour), inclusive (use smaller sub-groups to staff), and well organized by staff (objectives, agenda, minutes, action items, follow-up). There are usually just two reasons for a formal sit-down interagency meeting (as opposed to an interagency memorandum, tele-conference or "water-cooler" discussions). One is to reach and formalize *a decision* on a matter that requires the principals to agree, and the other is to hold an *exchange of technical information* with guest speakers and visuals that are not conducive to a memorandum.

If an interagency activity is important enough to discuss and reach an operations-bearing decision, then it is incumbent on the organizers to prepare the participants beforehand. A decision meeting should be prefaced days before by a "discussion paper" laying out background, discussion, pro-and-con arguments, and the chair's recommendation(s) on the issue. If the process is handled properly, positions will be discussed "off-line" and the decision meeting will be merely a formality to memorialize the decision—and save lots of time.

If the meeting or conference is to exchange information (some call these TEMs—Technical Exchange Meetings), then the same type of organization should precede it. Many small TEMs can often be handled by a memorandum with instructions to submit comments to a central place. Don't forget to follow-up with participants.

What's a "turf war?"

"Turf wars" usually occur when agency or department authorities overlap either legally (similar codes/statutes) or have the same geographic areas of responsibility (territories). A classic example was the recent and contentious debate between the Drug Enforcement Administration (DEA), and the FBI, and later the Immigration and Customs Enforcement agency (ICE). All had Title 21 USC (the federal Controlled Substance Act) drug enforcement powers. Who then had primacy? If a kilo of cocaine fell off a truck on a highway, who investigates? And let's not forget the S/Ls who also have state drug/narcotics enforcement statutes. A real potential donnybrook.

A casual observer might say, let the one who gets there first take charge. Actually, today, protocols for "who's in charge" have been worked out between the agencies to determine jurisdiction in cases such as the one above. Circumstances dictating who has the best chance of success in investigating and prosecuting the case are discussed and a lead agency is determined. If there is no agreement, the District United States Attorney and the district, county or state prosecutors would make the ultimate call. At least that is the way it is supposed to work. But let's face it, we are all flawed animals. I still wouldn't want to be the one trying to wrestle the "kilo" away from the State Police if they got there first.

Usually, a "turf war" can be avoided by aggressive interagency training and protocols, something that was still lacking with the Christmas Bomber incident of 2009. It is a pity, but it will not surprise the cynics to hear that many basic academies or training schools for homeland security-related officials do not include references to the respective missions of fellow interagency partners—It is always a work-in-progress.

Let's take the different missions of individual law enforcement and intelligence agencies as an example of basic misunderstanding. The end-game, *raison detre,* or basic goal of a law enforcement agency is to protect the public, and to do that it must catch, prosecute and punish criminals; while the mission of the federal intelligence community (IC) that is not part of a law enforcement agency, is to produce a "nugget" of strategic intelligence that might, just might, effect policies, procedures or operation planning—*that* is their "end-game." Compromising a valuable source of information to convict a dangerous criminal will not easily resonate with an Intel-type. Neither does allowing a criminal to operate freely so that "intelligence" about a subject can be gleaned make any sense to a lawman. Recognizing the different missions of the individual agencies will keep them from talking past each other. Why this basic piece of the "cultural puzzle" is not routinely force-fed into the education of emergency responders and intelligence officials working on homeland security remains a mystery.

"Turf wars" are the result of ignorance and arrogance.

Who are the main partners in a state's homeland security program?

As previously mentioned, on the state government side, the governor and members of the governor's office are key partners. The governor has a Chief Counsel and a Chief of Staff, both of whom are important and need to plug into any state emergency planning. Then, there is the Public Information Officer, who will need an effective response for the public during an emergency. Finally, there is usually an established cabinet-level homeland security council or task force.

In New Jersey, for example, the cabinet-level group is statutorily-driven. The "NJ Domestic Security Preparedness Task Force" is chaired by the governor's Homeland Security Advisor. The main members include the Attorney General, Superintendent of the State Police, the Adjutant General of the National Guard, the Treasurer, Commissioner (Secretary) of Health, Commissioner (Secretary) of Transportation, and three representatives from the private sector. *De facto,* other Cabinet members are included as appropriate, and still others as the subject matter requires. As previously mentioned, when in doubt, err on the side of inclusiveness.

For continuity (one Administration to the next), such a group should be formally established, preferably by passing a state law but an Executive Order issued by a governor can be more expedient. The directive should also establish an interagency executive group, i.e., second-level representatives of the principals' group. It is at the "seconds" group where the vetting work gets done on proposals and recommendations. Depending on issue, experts from government, academia, or the private sector may be asked to join. In other words, participation is dictated by the agenda.

What determines the makeup of private sector partners?

Most private or public partners are determined by the level of risk to a particular sector, but political and economic influence in the region cannot be ignored (see Chapter 4). For example, in the New Jersey/ New York City region, no serious discussion of homeland security is possible without the inclusion of the New York-New Jersey Port Authority, the New York Police Department, and the New Jersey Transit Authority. Academia is also a powerful ally; although effective use of such talent needs to be harnessed more efficiently through individual agreements with the appropriate institution—another challenge for the future. Most emergencies in the region will involve large agencies or businesses and their missions need to be taken into account in response planning. The same rationale applies to select critical infrastructure and key resources (CIKR), which need to be protected (see Chapter 5). Likewise, representatives from neighboring states form a part of a larger interagency group, again depending on the agenda.

In other words, institutionalizing participation of the key partners is important in the interagency process. But, <u>the most important factor to success is high-level leadership</u>. Everyone knows that if the boss places his or her imprimatur on the subject, it has to be important.

Chapter 3

Information Sharing Programs

As previously mentioned, deficiencies in information sharing among responsible agencies was a major finding of the 9/11 Commission, and correcting these deficiencies was their number one recommendation. They concluded that certain federal agencies had information before 9/11/2001 that, if shared, may have averted the terrorist events that unfolded that day. That charge was a huge indictment on the efficiency of the security forces protecting the homeland.

As it turns out, just as huge is implementing solutions to rectify what to an outsider seems uncomplicated. Ideally, the process is supposed to work this way: An authorized agency, as part of its duties, routinely collects information on, say, suspicious criminal activity, and that report gets distributed to every other agency that needs-to-know. Simple enough.

So, what's the problem?

Well, it is not one problem, but a myriad of technical and human complexities including an inordinately high volume of data contained in proprietary databases.

In this chapter, we will not discuss or refer to the operations of the federal effort, led primarily by the intelligence community (IC), which routinely deals with classified sensitive sources and methods affecting national security. Suffice it to say that improving *federal* sharing of information among them is an ongoing subject, which the media relentlessly probes, and which is being addressed by those responsible for administering and authorizing this vital effort.

What we will discuss is how states handle the wide range of security data encountered by the hundreds of thousands of domestic agencies, and what procedures are in place to collect, analyze and disseminate this data. Many believe it is this domestic synthesis of data that stands the best chance of thwarting the next terrorist plot.

Can you give a "real-world" example of "domestic synthesis of data?"

Let's say that an individual parked alongside the New Jersey Turnpike photographing parts of the Newark airport receives a written warning by a New Jersey State trooper for being illegally parked. *The man claimed he was a tourist.* A week later, the same individual is questioned and released by a New York/New Jersey Port Authority police officer, who observed the person taking photos of the Brooklyn Bridge's superstructure. *The man claims he is an architect.* Two weeks before either incident, the same individual entered the country through a land border crossing from Canada and gave his destination to the Immigration and Customs Enforcement official as a community college in Detroit, Michigan. *He claimed to be a student.* In each case, the official interviewing the person did a criminal and Intelligence Center name check, found no antecedents and filed a written field report of the contact, which was entered into a local electronic database. The three database systems are not routinely linked to each other, and so no alert was flagged on the subject. The contact information is considered "raw" data and is stored only in local databases because it does not pass a legal test as "intelligence."

Run that by me again?

Each incident described above, on its own, is not enough to be considered worthy of investigative follow-up attention. Such actions are commonplace, but regardless, a record is made and stored in a local system. Many believe that, in fact, that is where you will find most of the infamous "dots" that people casually claim need to be connected. There are many "infractions" like traffic tickets or running your dog off a leash in a restricted area that do not warrant a second look on face value. And even if S/Ls had the resources, which they don't, that type of information does not meet the "reasonable suspicion" threshold required for input into an "intelligence" collection data systems.

The synthesis of this type of data, however, is the challenge faced by state homeland security officials. To connect "dots," you first have to collect them. If the individual mentioned above had acted more suspiciously, say he had no identification or tried to flee and had been formally arrested, that activity would have automatically "pinged" an Intelligence Center somewhere. Fusion Centers and FBI JTTFs have improved dramatically in linking suspicious data. But linking the individual record management systems (RMS) of S/Ls continues to be a major challenge.

So, is this a technical challenge?

Not entirely. There are other obstacles, such as funding. Very few S/Ls can afford to re-tool their current RMSs to conform to regional systems. Centralization of data can be expensive. There are also legal and protocol considerations. A tourist taking pictures of an airport or bridge should not have to worry about turning up in a "terrorist watch list." Sharing individual RMSs with other agencies can generate civil rights concerns, privacy issues, and proprietary questions. Once an individual's name is entered into a police record, there may be no way to purge that name later or keep that information separate from other data housed in the local RMS. These non-technical questions are being worked by state fusion centers.

Are law enforcement agencies cooperating on this effort?

That is a definite, yes. One development that has made a major difference in the level of cooperation is that law enforcement agencies (LEAs) now see a clear nexus between routine crime information and the information that analysts need (the "dots") to stitch together a possible terrorist threat or pattern. You see, the greater threats faced daily by most LEAs, especially in the larger cities, are drugs, gangs, and violence. Counterterrorism information is often buried among the greater body of criminal information, and counterterrorism experts have to recognize that information-sharing and any level of cooperation with LEAs is based on working within that LEA threat priority. LEAs and counterterrorism experts alike recognize that investigating stolen cars, fraudulent documents, illegal weapons, drug trafficking and other violence-supporting crimes can also be related to preventing acts of terrorism. A robber, burglar and terrorist all do surveillance before the crime. So, that tourist taking pictures bears noting. This philosophy is being injected into current LEA training.

Where do the private sector and the public enter into the information sharing effort?

Good question. Although the *9/11 Commission Report* focused on Intelligence agencies and law enforcement agencies not sharing information, states face a broader challenge. The flow of information needs to include the public and the private sector if they are to draw on the vigilance and resources at the disposal of homeland security and preparedness efforts.

And this flow of information has to be in both directions. We have discussed the merits of inclusiveness in the previous chapter and the same applies to information sharing. A state counterterrorism and disaster preparedness strategy has to include the public and private sector as full partners in that enterprise. Joint training and exercises, town hall meetings at the county and municipal levels, Chamber of Commerce and business conferences all lend themselves as opportunities to engage the public and key businesses.

Information sharing sounds like a law enforcement-centric effort. Is that true?

LEAs are naturally comfortable in security environments, but when it comes to public outreach and disaster preparedness efforts, the entire emergency response community (ERC) has to be brought to bear, especially the fire service, which often gets overlooked in this effort. Fire Departments are widely dispersed and in most neighborhoods. Within some communities, firefighters have strong public followings that can be very useful when communicating information on public preparedness. The same is true for medical emergency services and other responders. Using the entire ERC as full partners in sharing information with other responders and the public is becoming a common practice. As full members of the fusion centers, members of the ERC are now active in disseminating information in many states.

How is the public plugged into these programs?

Most states have individual websites for their respective Office of Emergency Management (OEM) and their offices of homeland security and preparedness, which can be easily found using an Internet search engine. These sites contain considerable information about disaster planning and links to related agencies that contain further invaluable information on emergencies. Although not as tailored to localities, federal emergency offices and departments such as DHS, FEMA, Health, Transportation and others also have information that the public can "pull" from websites.

During emergencies, however, much of the information has to be "pushed" to, and retrieved from, agencies and the public by the local ERC. For that purpose, many states have set up individual programs. In New Jersey, for example, many counties, municipalities, and private businesses have set up a "reverse 9-1-1," an automated calling system that will "push" information to subscribers. 2-1-1 (used in some states) is an easy phone number to remember and it allows a caller to talk to an operator (not automated), who has the latest credible information on a given emergency or situation. Local emergency websites will tell you what is available in your area.

What if the public wants to discuss a situation involving possible terrorism but for non-attribution?

When it comes to sharing information on suspected terrorism, many states have set up a separate phone number, usually a 1-800 or 1-866 line, where a caller can discuss suspicious activity with a specialist (usually a retired law enforcement officer). These information call centers are tailored to the state needs and are not duplicative from the federal "See Something Say Something" campaigns that are being propagated regionally. Many states have merged this public service with an all-crimes "hot" line. Note: This calling system is not a substitute for the 9-1-1, which is still the recognized number to call for emergencies. We'll discuss "Tips and Leads" phone lines separately in Chapter 6. Tips and Leads phone lines are the lynch-pin to communicating unsolicited terrorism-related information between the public, S/Ls and the FBI.

Most LEA websites will post brochures, such as "The Seven Signs of Terrorism" or like information that the public can use as guides. These are available upon request from counterterrorism offices at Police Department's and Prosecutor's Offices. If they haven't done so, an agency might consider putting them at fire houses.

Suffice it to say that a well-informed public is a formidable ally in the disaster prevention and preparedness effort.

Chapter 4

Risk-based Management and
Decision Making

As we have already described, state homeland security and preparedness efforts are diverse and managed by countless S/L authorities under the leadership of the governor and his or her homeland security advisor. It is their responsibility to set priorities and manage initiatives accordingly, despite the challenge of limited budgets. Federal grant funds are extremely helpful in these cases, but they are usually programmed as "seed money" (short term stimulus—enough to get you started), and always have conditions.

When it comes to federal grants (see Chapter 9), local budgets have to account for out-year costs. For example, even if the federal government were to give you a trained bomb-sniffing canine and provide the training for the handler free of charge, you would still have to dedicate a full-time-employee with salary, benefits, and maintenance costs to deploy the team.

Likewise, the private sector has to prioritize and manage security funding. Most companies view security programs as "overhead costs," (i.e., right off the top of the profits line). As a result, these entities tend to spend only what they feel is necessary or mandated by code. It takes vision for an agency to make a business-case for investing in disaster preparedness planning.

Furthermore, it seems there is no public priority for investments in all-hazard preparedness, even where disasters are known to happen frequently. For example, a recent Harvard University study found that

30% of people living along the coast from Brownsville, Texas to Myrtle Beach, South Carolina stated that they would *not* evacuate their homes if ordered by authorities to do so on the eve of a hurricane.

Such complacency is difficult to manage. Prioritizing and confidence building become key.

How does a company or an agency determine what is "justified and necessary?"

They do it the same way an actuary (a person who calculates probabilities) does it to figure out insurance risks, and thereby, premiums (See Table 1)—despite the public's apathy. No one along the New Jersey shore, for example, believes a hurricane is going to hit them because the last hurricane of any consequence was a hundred years ago. They don't want to even hear that a strong hurricane directly hitting the shore will level the terrain two miles inland (and kill anyone within that path) because they feel that the probability is slim, if not unrealistic. In cases like these, there is no way to convince taxpayers to justify expenditures to constantly plan and exercise a private or public response.

Meanwhile, it is the responsibility of homeland security experts and planners to address a potential threat to the homeland and to assess the risks involved and the consequences of not taking precautions. You don't get invited to too many cocktail parties when discussing "doom and gloom" scenarios is part your repertoire.

How can you systematically make priority assessments?

Like an actuary who uses probability models, a homeland security analyst assesses risk. You have to accept that risk is calculated by assessing threats, vulnerabilities and consequences.

RISK = THREAT + VULNERABILITY + CONSEQUENCE

There are many variations and applications of this model to calculate risk. To better understand and tailor the calculation needed, you'll have to ascertain what is accepted or known about each component. Then, you have to quantify the value you place on each. For example, you are the owner of a chemical company that stores toxic chemicals in a densely populated area. Since chemicals have been used by terrorists as a weapon, even though there may not be a direct threat to your company, there is a high implied *threat* (either to steal chemicals or to use the facility itself as a target) that you need to weigh. If your company is not protected like Fort Knox then there is a *high* likelihood that a bomb can be introduced inside your facility—you are *vulnerable*. If that bomb were detonated, that would result a high level of *consequence* to life and property. When all three factors are rated "high," you can easily conclude that the risk is great and you had better invest in a strategy to mitigate that risk. It is not often, however, that all three components will rate high simultaneously.

Assessments can also vary greatly by region. In the mid-Atlantic states, for example, the "threat" aspect of risk resonates *high* because of 9/11 and because Washington, DC and the New York City region are favorite targets, if not *the* top targets, for foreign and domestic terrorists, by their own admission.

How is the "risk-based model" applied in decision-making?

Most executives today support and utilize risk-based management in making homeland security decisions. Unfortunately, the "dash-for-the-cash" (federal grant monies, see Chapter 9) has produced some skewed regional assessments. At one time, Wyoming, *per capita*, was receiving more federal homeland security dollars than New York City. Fortunately, the federal government has since corrected that imbalance and is applying a more sensible risk-based approach. But, regional posturing around the country will continue to effect priority assessments when it comes to federal grants dollars.

Do the States use risk based assessments?

The states use a form of the risk-based model to re-distribute resources and dollars. Each state appoints a State Administrative Agent (SAA), who is responsible for managing and distributing grant funds. When risks are correctly identified, articulated and funding properly audited, stakeholder and the public should not have complaints about being short-changed.

The same decision-making practices apply to shoring up security among the private sector, even though some security experts believe that many CEOs are still not engaged. In the next chapter, we will discuss government and private sector partnerships, but it is worth re-enforcing here that CEOs and company administrators use risk-based management to decide how much resources and funding to apply to security. In the mid-Atlantic region, making a "business-case" for the security of employees and neighbors should not be a problem for executives. Even during tough economic times, people in this region will take the images of the Twin Towers, the Pentagon and Shanksville to their graves, and will support strong government to insure there is no repetition. But, they will not tolerate making the same mistakes again and again.

Does the federal government use risk-based assessments?

For the most part it does. Our discussions here are focused on state decision-making. Still, some reference to federal applications is appropriate.

Every state produces a homeland security and preparedness state-of-the-state report, either formally or informally. The federal government requires states to contribute to the National Infrastructure Protection Plan (NIPP)[6], which has a segment devoted to Risk Assessment, and also adds a "resiliency" component as an update item to this year's version. We'll discuss Critical Infrastructure Protection more in Chapter 8. But, we note here that the federal government collaborates with the states in developing risk assessments for critical infrastructure. For the most part, states develop their own assessments for planning purposes. In the high-risk areas of the country, the S/L risk-based focus is strong and credible. In other areas, the effort is less so.

---

[6]   2009 National Infrastructure Protection Plan—Partnering to Enhance Protection and Resiliency Department of Homeland Security—2009

Can the federal government overrule a state assessment?

In high-risk sections of the country, this is unlikely. State attention to assessments and compliance with the NIPP are strong and the federal government concedes that S/Ls in these areas know more about their areas of responsibility than they do. In low-risk areas or sectors, S/Ls invest little in these assessments and look to the feds for early notifications of possible threats. In most of these areas the term "risk" and the term "threat" are used interchangeably.

Table 1: How an Actuary Views Risk[7]

- **Offsetting one risk with another.** Under certain circumstances, two harmful events might possess the characteristic that when the likelihood of one goes up, the likelihood of the other goes down. Thus, if we know that when coffee prices go up, soda prices go down, we might want to invest in both coffee and soda stocks, to manage our risk.

- **Risk is a matter of perspective.** What might be harmful to one party, might be good for another. For example, when the value of the dollar goes down against the French Franc, which might be bad for an American business, but favorable for a French business. By trading off the consequences of an undesirable event with another party who is affected favorably, both parties are made better off.

- **Focus on catastrophic risks.** Mathematical theory shows that the greatest relief from risk (and consequently, the greatest increase in peace of mind) comes from eliminating the consequences of events that are very unlikely, but result in very big losses. Thus, families should think about what might happen if the breadwinner dies, their house

---

[7]   Society of Actuaries, Casualty Actuarial Society website, www.beanactuary. com

burns down, or they lose all of their savings. They should then implement solutions that reduce the likelihood of these events, as well as manage their financial impact. This might involve purchasing a life insurance policy or investing the savings in many different stocks, to reduce the exposure to any one company's fortunes. Generally, a few simple measures taken to address catastrophic risks have a great impact on our well-being.

• __Diversify, diversify, diversify__. It is better to take on many small risks than face one big risk. Many small risks generally average out, to give an outcome that is not too extreme in one direction or another. Results become more predictable. Thus, diversification is an important tool in managing risk.

Chapter 5

Public/Private Partnerships

If you are relying on *only* government security agencies to secure the homeland, you have your head stuck in the proverbial sand. It was only back in ancient, homogenous times when groups of like-minded individuals would agree to salary, train, and authorize "centurions" to protect society from the deviants among them. Or as the grey beards call them: the good-ole-days.

Some will say that it was the industrial revolution, or the advent of global travel and commerce, or a series of modernization that have made the world smaller and as a result more dangerous. Nevertheless, wars and tribal conflicts have been a fixture throughout history. Whatever the reason—possibly the sheer number of people that can be affected by modern day events—we all agree that today public safety, especially against natural and man-made disasters, overwhelms the efforts of those charged with insuring that we live and work in the safest environment possible. Therefore, in order to be effective, our public policy on prevention and preparedness efforts, *must* include the private sector and the general public.

Is that being done?

Not as assuredly as some security experts would want, but yes, inclusion of public and private sector is recognized by policy planners as an essential component of homeland security. At the national level, this partnership is under-scored in all of the missions of DHS. Whether agencies are enhancing security against terrorism, securing our borders, enforcing immigration laws, safeguarding cyberspace, or ensuring resilience (the five DHS missions), the private sector, especially life-sustaining infrastructure, plays a most important role. Keep in mind that 85 to 90 percent of our critical infrastructure is owned and administered by the private sector.

States include education as a critical resource and part of hometown security, both for prevention and preparedness efforts. Schools and campuses of higher education are as safe as the local planning and response plans between educators and law enforcement are strong. The same applies to other industrial complexes, such as entertainment and shopping malls. With the advent of foreign terrorists targeting the homeland, the immediacy to institutionalize and strengthen these partnerships has greatly increased. Every state should recognize this fact. In high-risk areas such as New Jersey, New York, and Washington D.C., protocols (standardized rules to follow) have been legislated; they recognize this partnership as part of their offices of homeland security and emergency management.

What do you mean by "private sector?"

The simple answer is, any industry or institution that is privately owned and operated, as opposed to public agencies, such as government agencies or institutions paid for by tax dollars. As mentioned earlier, 85-90% of our critical infrastructure and key resources are in the hands of the private sector. The National Infrastructure Protection Plan (NIPP), previously mentioned, identifies the Critical Infrastructure and Key Resources (CIKR) having highest homeland security priority. We'll discuss these more in Chapter 8, but they include:

Agriculture and Food; Defense Industrial Base; Energy, Healthcare and Public Health; National Monuments and Icons; Banking and Finance; Chemical Commercial Facilities; Critical Manufacturing; Dams; Emergency Services; Nuclear Reactors, Materials and Waste; Information Technology; Communications; Postal and Shipping; Transportation Systems; and Government Facilities.

Most states would add *Entertainment* and *Education* to their list of key resources and, although they are not directly "life-sustaining," the states' Offices of Emergency Management (OEM) would certainly include them in any protection and preparedness plan. The reasons for this inclusion are the large number of people who gather in "open" environments (unrestricted access) and the schooling activities of our most cherished resource—our children.

Is "collaboration" and "partnership" the same thing?

No, and that is a good point to make. "Collaboration" refers to people, agencies, entities interacting to discuss solutions to problems and make recommendations for actions. An interagency "task force" to look into proposed policy or procedural changes is an example. A "partnership" refers to people, agencies or entities that organize with each other to *implement* changes or take certain actions together.

Is the private sector cooperating with this "partnership" approach?

Again, it varies by area and the collaboration tends to be with their own kind, but for the most part, yes; you do not get much of an argument from them on the general premise. Continuity of business operations is more their model and they are quite focused when it comes to preparedness. Large corporations and businesses, especially those that might be terrorist targets, do not need government regulations to plan and cooperate in the spirit of regulations and "best business practice;" they get it. What large industries and businesses occasionally "do not get" is the lack of state government standardization in compliance rules across the country. Trade organizations representing industry can be very diligent about participating in public policy discussions, and states, for the most part, are amenable. Both recognize that enhancing safety and security practices is in everyone's interest. Visionary companies do see the wisdom (business case) of partnering with government agencies in disaster planning. Unfortunately, there are still some companies that ignore a partnership approach because they are parochial in their thinking and fear regulation, or just plain greedy.

How can homeland security agencies manage such a diverse landscape?

The answer is simpler than you might think. "Home-rule" can be used to an advantage in these cases. Public and private leaders, such as a city mayor and the major employers in the region, probably already know each other (if they don't, one or both of them is not doing his or her job). The same applies to top law enforcement or fire services officials and superintendents of school districts, and so forth. It is good governance and business practice for community leaders to get to know each other. The smaller the community, the more collegial the relationship can be. Homeland security should be a topic of discussion and an agenda item of community meetings, from budget hearings to Chamber of Commerce meetings. Pretty basic stuff.

What about public perception to these partnerships?

The public is more understanding than some give it credit. You don't need much of a reason to garner their attention on homeland security, if you are inclined to be proactive. Consider the following: When it comes to terrorism or natural disasters, there are daily headline news incidents around the globe; our young service men and women are currently fighting overseas; your state's National Guard was federalized and deployed to Iraq during that war a multitude of times; and often that disaster on the 6 O'clock news has a local connection. A tsunami or hurricane somewhere, a Columbine-type active-shooter in some U.S. city, an attack on a religious institution is some sleepy town, a tragedy that is reported somewhere on the 6 O'clock news, any of these events have local relevance. How? Such an event does not have to hit your community before you can have a discussion about prevention and preparedness of such events.

A homeland security official can (and should) seize these opportunities to engage the public in discussions about local preparedness: What if that (fill in the event) had happened here? Are we prepared? How can you, the public or private business, help? Explain what the state has currently planned or organized in case such an event had happened here. Again, as we've emphasized before, a well-informed public is a formidable ally.

Can public/private collaboration and partnerships be institutionalized?

Yes they can. For example, in New Jersey, the statute which governs the state's policy and planning for homeland security and preparedness, requires three private sector representatives on that body. Likewise, DHS routinely includes private sector representatives on advisory boards and councils. It can get a bit tricky when the information or policy subject matter involves a national security activity or criminal prosecution, which requires compartmentalization, but these issues can be addressed proactively by either obtaining clearances for those representatives who have a need to know, or sanitizing the classified parts. In most cases, policy and preparedness discussions do not involve that degree of granularity.

No one questions the logic of institutionalizing public and private partnerships. The question is, how well are these encounters planned and organized? Are protocols for notification and inclusion during emergencies exercised and followed routinely? After Katrina, for example, the state of Mississippi called Bell South to assist in emergency communications. That arrangement worked fine. However, during the same disaster, the food industry was not called upon or engaged systematically to help feed the region. The government should not have to stockpile food and water for emergencies when the food industry knows best how to store and distribute that commodity. But, such arrangements and agreements have to be considered, organized and exercised *before* the disaster strikes. As a result of lessons-learned from Katrina, many states have formalized pacts with the private sector for capabilities such as food distribution during emergencies. It is up to individual state leadership to insure the highest level of representation and priority for these partnerships.

Chapter 6

Fusion Centers—Domestic Counterterrorism

First some definitions:

Fusion—To turn information and intelligence into actionable knowledge.[8]

Fusion Centers—An effective and efficient mechanism to exchange information and intelligence, maximize resources, streamline operations, and improve the ability to fight crime and terrorism by analyzing data from a variety of sources.[9]

Fusion Process—Collection, analysis and dissemination of terrorism-related intelligence. The overarching process of managing the flow of information and intelligence across all levels and sectors of government and private industry.[10]

A historical perspective: The idea of interagency information sharing centers is not new. Expediency creates them when a security threat demands an interagency "task force" approach to collect, analyze and disseminate the best information. It is not difficult to organize; you simply populate a central location (center) with representatives from each agency having relevant information. The individual representatives can

---

[8]   Fusion Center Guidelines—Developing and Sharing Information and Intelligence in a New Era, August 2006, U.S. Department of Homeland Security, U.S. Department of Justice
[9]   *Ibid*
[10] *Ibid*

then access their respective information and share it, under established rules, with other members, and initiate the fusion process.

The popularity of such fusion centers reached a crest during the so-called "war on drugs" in the mid-80s. Interagency centers such as the El Paso Intelligence Center (EPIC), the National Drug Intelligence Center (NDIC), and numerous state and regional crime Intelligence Centers were formed to facilitate the operational information needs of the law enforcement community.

Fusion centers in the post 9/11 era were started as a joint project between the Department of Homeland Security and the U.S. Department of Justice's Office of Justice Programs between 2003 and 2007.

How are fusion centers different today?

Today, the federal law enforcement focus is on counterterrorism, and there is also a need to involve the private sector. As a result, several key functions are included in some of today's S/L fusion centers. As we previously mentioned, to "connect the dots" on terrorism-related information you need a comprehensive review from various sources of information including "all-crimes." The advantage to law enforcement agencies is obvious. After all, the purpose of fusing data collectively is to disseminate an all-source information product, either as a time-sensitive "pointer" to interested agencies about a possible criminal event, or as a piece of analyzed information, or, as it's called in the business, intelligence. The fusion process can apply to terrorism as well as other crimes.

Another benefit of the fusion centers today is that agencies can have a central location to report and retrieve sensitive information. This function is more beneficial when agencies are smaller and spread out. Larger LEAs have their own Intelligence Units. Often emergency dispatching is attached to a fusion center as well as other activities, such as a "call center" where the public can report "tips and leads," or the center can house Offices of Emergency Management (OEMs) or even double as an Emergency Operating Center (EOC) for state emergencies. In some states, the fusion center also houses all of these functions for the state and the state police.

Since 9/11, there has been a proliferation of S/L fusion centers—over 60 at last count. Most are subsidized by DHS and follow DHS guidelines. These guidelines recognize that each fusion center has unique characteristics, but *it is important for centers to operate under a consistent framework—similar to the construction of a group of buildings where each structure is unique yet a consistent set of building codes and regulations are adhered to regardless of the size and shape of the building.*[11]

It is the intention of DHS to use these centers as a means to disseminate information, as well as a means to glean regional data. For this purpose, DHS assigns personnel to select centers, and the states, in turn, often assign officials to DHS' Office of Intelligence and Analysis (I & A).

How important are state fusion centers?

These centers ultimately hold the key to meeting the information-sharing challenge, which, as we discussed, remains a work in progress. They have added considerable value in drug enforcement efforts. An example happened years ago when aggressive enforcement by the New York Police Department (NYPD) forced certain ethnic drug traffickers to leave New York and re-locate their criminal activity to Philadelphia and Boston. Analysts from the various departments discovered that Philadelphia and Boston had certain characteristics attractive to those groups, such as similar ethnic neighborhoods, access to international airports and interstate highways, and certain other local advantages. Then, the analysts quickly asked: Where else are these traits found? As it turned out, Charlotte, North Carolina and Columbus, Ohio did. This fusion of information led to warning notices to authorities there, and parts in between, that they could expect criminal activity to spread there soon, and provided them with mug shots, fingerprints, and methods

---

[11]   *Ibid*

of operation of possible suspects. These groups never established themselves in Charlotte and Columbus. Fusion works.

Modern fusion centers have incorporated at least these four tactics and understandings to better assess and respond to the everyday threats to the homeland.

a) **Tips and Leads Programs**

Most states tailor a "Tips 'n Leads" program to rally the public to report anomalies about suspected terrorist-related activities. Much effort is made to educate the public to look for the "signs of terrorism," and as a result, this reporting mechanism was developed. In most states, a 1-866 number was established to accommodate a public vigilance campaign. Slogans, such as "If you see something, say something," or "The greatest defense against terrorism is YOU," have been publicized on billboards and media. Calls from the public average about a hundred per month in most states (considerably more following a publicized terrorist event anywhere in the country).

A dynamic area that is catching on quickly is the monitoring and analysis of open source information, as found on the Internet and the various public social medias. Properly managed and sorted, blogs and real-time texting, can provide tips and leads that are invaluable. Many fusion centers are monitoring Twitter and other texting media programs to obtain first-hand information of emergencies. Private companies and industry are also using social media programs to better reach personnel and elicit information from them.

Tips and Leads program reports are screened by trained specialists and forwarded to the appropriate authorities (usually the FBI) for further investigation. If the caller is not anonymous, specialists make it a point to call the person back at a later time and provide a general status, if appropriate.

In at-risk states, these programs have already paid dividends. The "Fort Dix Six" case is a good example of a citizen's tip being developed into a full-blown investigation. A vigilant film store attendant noticed what he thought was suspicious activity on film he developed for a customer. Unsure of what he had, he called the local police who in turn spoke to a specialist from the New Jersey Office of Homeland Security and Preparedness, who in turn forwarded the information to the FBI. Following a year-long investigation by the FBI Joint Terrorism Task Force in Philadelphia, in 2008 the suspects were arrested, charged and convicted for plotting to kill members of the U.S. military at Fort Dix.

The public is invaluable in "connecting dots."

b) Intelligence Units—Strategic vs. Tactical

The most accepted way of organizing an Intelligence Unit is to break up staff into geographic and specific crime areas or "desks." A state can define its own "area of responsibility" map, or it can use existing boundaries, such as counties, major cities, or congressional districts. Analysts can also be assigned to different crime specialties, e.g., robbery, car theft, homicide, terrorism, etc. As intelligence products are developed, the interaction of the various geographic and functional "desks" becomes the catalyst that fuses the information into intelligence.

Note: Intelligence products fall into two basic categories: <u>tactical</u> and <u>strategic</u>.

A simple "rule of thumb" is:

1. If the analysis is deemed actionable (supporting an operation), it is "tactical" intelligence,
2. If the analysis predicts an emerging trend or pattern, it is "strategic" intelligence.

c) State and Local Intelligence "Communities of Interest"

It is the goal of DHS to establish Homeland Security state and Local Intelligence Community of Interest (HS SLIC) in all of the state fusion centers, and become a key element of the National Fusion Center Network. What that means is that S/L analysts can link with DHS and each other through a secure Internet portal and share sensitive homeland security intelligence, information and analyzes on a daily basis. The program has been successfully tested in six states—Arizona, California, Florida, Illinois, New York and Virginia.

d) FBI Joint Terrorism Task Forces (JTTFs)

JTTFs also have Intelligence Units that work in a classified environment, and are the bridge between the S/Ls and the federal Intelligence Community. The JTTF program is designed to include cleared S/L representatives, who are assigned to FBI squads as equal partners on terrorism-related investigations. Through the JTTF, the relationship between the S/L fusion centers and the FBI has grown and is mutually beneficial. Often a personnel exchange program between the state fusion center and the JTTF is helpful, especially when activity is brisk.

Any down-side to fusion centers?

There is nothing wrong with the fusion center concept, but ultimately, agencies contributing either information or personnel will need to see the value-added. Information from the fusion centers will have to routinely help the S/L law enforcement community do its daily policing more effective, and that effectiveness will have to be measurable and attested to by the police departments themselves. Let's not forget the "human interoperability" factor. Unless fusion centers receive this value-added endorsement, S/L participation, which is critical, will wane, and the fusion will fizzle.

Is that likely to happen?

Right now, no. Mainly, because DHS is re-emphasizing the value of the centers as hubs for exchanging information with S/L agencies and the private sector, and federal funds are being applied to this effort. DHS also recognizes the value of the centers for local "situational awareness," namely, as a local knowledge-base. Who knows best what the local risks, priorities, limitations and capabilities are than the locals? Fusion centers can provide this information routinely if properly instructed and tasked. Recommendations are currently being developed to make that service a "deliverable" (a tasking or requirement) in exchange for federal funding.

How is success measured?

A synthesis of nationwide and regional information could produce crime and terrorism intelligence that is both tactical (operational) and strategic (trends and patterns) and that would give S/Ls "early warning" about a threat in their area. That would be viewed even by the most cynical S/L as value-added. Overcoming strong feelings by some S/Ls that the information and resource flow to these centers is a "one-way street" has to be a short-term goal if fusion centers are to survive.

Chapter 7

State Offices of Emergency Management (OEMs) and Emergency Operations Centers (EOCs)

If you were to break down the activities that surround state homeland security programs, they would fall into two baskets: *Prevention* and *Preparedness*.

See Figure 2

Prevention	Preparedness
✓ Counterterrorism	✓ Natural and man-made Disasters
✓ Law Enforcement and Intelligence	✓ Office of Emergency Management
✓ Joint Terrorism Task Forces	✓ Emergency Response Community
✓ Fusion Centers	✓ Emergency Operations Centers
✓ Intelligence Community	✓ Critical Infrastructure Protection
✓ Information Sharing	✓ Resiliency

Fig 2 - Focus

What exactly is an Emergency Operations Center (EOC)?

An EOC is a central command and control facility responsible for carrying out disaster management functions in an emergency situation and ensuring the continuity of operations, both government and the private sector. Just as work places are required to have building evacuation plans for emergencies, disaster planning includes items such as identifying "essential personnel" to maintain continuity of critical operations, and their "credentialing," that is, a system that provides the necessary certification, recognized by security personnel, that allows employees access to an essential work places during disasters. One of the lessons from Katrina was that even with exercising, emergency personnel will see to the needs of their families first. Maintaining command and control of disaster response is critical. The EOC is the hub for that activity.

When activated, state EOC facilities bring together decision-makers and authorities into an interconnected environment to prioritize and dispatch response to disasters. The activities of the emergency response community to a disaster in managed from the EOC. The objectives of the EOC are phased: Secure the disaster area (keep the situation from getting worse), see to the sick or injured, rescue survivors (save lives), and mitigate damage (stabilize and recover from effects).

State Office of Emergency Management (OEM)
What are the differences between OEM, EOC, ERC, FEMA??

Before you get overwhelmed with the "alphabet soup," consider Figure 3.

OEM	Office of Emergency Management	An Agency	State, Local, Tribal
EOC	Emergency Operations Center	A Facility	State, Local, Tribal
ERC	Emergency Response Community	An Interagency Body	Federal, State, Local, Tribal
FEMA	Federal Emergency Management Agency	An Agency	Federal

Fig. 3 Acronyms

State OEMs are staffed by full-time emergency planners from the ERC, and in turn, insure that EOCs are staffed and operate properly when activated. That requires OEMs to be involved in ERC daily activities and plan for disasters. The federal equivalent of a state OEM is the Federal Emergency Management Agency (FEMA). Clear as mud? Keep referring to Figure 3.

A major responsibility of OEMs is planning and preparedness for disasters and seeing to concomitant emergency training and exercises. State OEMs also have a responsibility to insure that smaller versions of county and city OEMs are included in disaster and emergency planning, especially since many of the large counties and municipalities across the country have individual EOC facilities.

In some states, the state's OEM is managed by the State Police and the EOC is located inside the state's fusion center.

Why so many versions of OEMs?

Natural and man-made disasters come in different sizes. Events range from emergencies that can affect a neighborhood to ones that can affect an entire country. It is said that all emergencies start local, and the emergency responders, made up of police, fire, medical, HazMat, utilities, etc., respond to them all, and on a daily basis. When emergency response exceeds local capabilities, the appropriate authority calls for an "emergency situation," which can be city-wide, county-wide, state-wide, or national in scope. When there are no pending emergencies, it is up to the individual OEMs to remain vigilant by prepare for them with exercises, training, and planning, the same as a peace-time military constantly prepares for war.

The purpose of preparedness programs, in general, led by state OEM agencies, *is to improve emergency management and preparedness capabilities by supporting flexible, sustainable, secure and interoperable EOCs with a focus on addressing identified deficiencies and needs.*[12] (This, admittedly, not-very-clear statement happens to outline the exact purpose of DHS' EOC Grant Program, word for word.) In clearer terms:

---

[12]   FEMA, FY-10 Guidelines for Emergency Operations Center Grants Program, Department of Homeland Security FY-10 Budget.

All of these agencies are designed to help improve response to an event and minimize or prevent initial damage.

There are five considerations that OEM preparedness planners need to reflect as part of their strategy for successfully countering and recovering from specific emergencies.

a) Volunteer Emergency Response Teams

Recent and past disasters have taught the ERC (the pros) the value of having a trained group of volunteers from the community at the ready to assist when needed. As we know, large disasters can easily overwhelm the ERC. Volunteer groups such as the Community Emergency Response Teams (CERTS) and Neighborhood Emergency Response Teams (NERTS) fall under the umbrella organization, Citizen Corps, which is funded in part by the Stafford Act,[13] and is federal law. CERTS and similar citizen-based organizations are managed locally by state OEMs.

Many states, including densely populated ones such as New Jersey and other mid-Atlantic states, are wholly dependent on volunteer fire and medical emergency services; in some cases, they make up as much as 80% of them. This number may surprise some people, but more alarming is the fact that recently the number of applicants is decreasing, volunteers are retiring, especially in "home-rule" states. State OEMs should examine this trend, and if applicable, launch a vigorous recruiting and retention campaign.

Again, as with other issues, partnership programs between local governments and the public are the

---

[13]   The Robert T. Stafford Disaster Relief and Emergency Assistance Act (Stafford Act), Pub. L. 100-707, 1988 amended version of the Disaster Relief Act of 1974, Pub. L. 93-288.

solution. Where these ERC partnerships are strong, emergency response is strong. Case in point: emergency evacuations.

b) Evacuations

Many factors contribute to successful evacuations. They include, public confidence in government leaders, early warning, exercising, and proper public/private interaction. Unfortunately, "successful evacuations" have not been the norm. As mentioned earlier, all recent studies indicate that faced with a pending Katrina-like hurricane, up to 30% of the public will not evacuate when ordered to do so. Reasons vary from bravado, not wanting to leave home or pets behind, complacency that "It's just not going to happen here," to plain curiosity. State OEMs and the ERC needs to invest in strong and timely public awareness campaigns, especially in at-risk areas. The aim is to convince people that when OEM asks them to leave (precautionary stage), or the governor orders them to leave (imminent emergency), they must act reasonably and precipitously. In this regard, posting evacuation routes and exercising various scenarios is a must.

Consider the following: The water surge from a Category 3 hurricane along the coast will flatten structures two miles inland, both going in and coming back out. Few in its wake will survive. *Want to see the photographs from Katrina?* And while "experts" may debate the probabilities of a Cat 3, 2 or 1 in this life-time hitting certain coastal areas, such as the Jersey Shore, disaster planners do not ignore the vulnerability and the consequences of such an event, nor should the residents. That IS a fact.

States affected by hurricanes, forest fires, flooding, snow storms and other disasters (*are any states exempt?*) that may require evacuations have to place a high priority on frequent exercises and make sure that departments such as Departments of Transportation, Health, and Environment, are not excluded. These exercises should also include the option of sheltering-in-place, which may be the best course of action depending on the circumstances.

c) Personal Disaster Kits

Sometimes called "go-bags" during emergency evacuations, these personal disaster kits consist of items such as official documents and other valuables that can be kept in a safe and central place where they can be accessed easily. During an emergency, you don't want to be rummaging through files for your important papers.

But, disaster kits also consist of preparedness items in case you need to shelter-in-place, as is the case following a nuclear event or when roads are impassable. Items such as food, water, first-aid kits, flashlights, batteries, medicines, and other contingency items should be kept in stock. States should insure that their OEM websites have examples of disaster kits posted and updated, along with a reminder to test them every so often—batteries do not last forever. FEMA recommends a three-day supply of such items, since in major disasters it may take that long for rescue or aid to arrive.

d) Disaster Medicine

The study and practice of disaster medicine, also called, *terror medicine*, has proliferated this past decade in the U.S., although a focus in many other countries prior to 9/11. And while examples of the need for terror medicine favors the threats posed by biological agents such as anthrax, the medical management of terrorist attacks involves a variety of other possible weapons. In fact, bombs and explosives have been the weapons most commonly used by terrorists and continues to draw the most attention, according to primers, such as The Essentials of Terror Medicine, by Drs. Shapira, Cole and Hammond.[14] Likewise, the Israeli government has offered to share its considerable medical response experience and research on the subject. Considerable references are also available in open-sources on the Internet.

Findings also confirm that medical response does not only involve specialization in treating bodily damage, but psychological effects as well. State preparedness experts have to take into account the fact that terror victims may have multiple types of body wounds, for example, or that taking multiple victims to the "nearest" hospital, as would be the case in conventional emergencies, will most likely overwhelm most medical centers during disasters, and that the trauma of a disaster, such as 9/11, reaches beyond the obvious and "touches" a multitude of "walking wounded," witnesses and even TV observers. Emergency response plans for the use of disaster medicine must include these provisions and adjust accordingly.

e) Campus/School Security

This subject is not usually found in preparedness plans by FEMA or most OEMs. However, states that have experienced the results of a murdering active-shooter loose on a campus or school (and I can think of Virginia, Pennsylvania and Colorado, right off the bat) can attest to nothing more "terrifying" when discussing *hometown* security emergencies. Add to that rationale the fact that

---

[14] *The Essentials of Terror Medicine*, Shmuel C. Shapira, Leonard Cole, Jeffery S. Hammond, September 2009, Springer Publishing

the chances of students encountering an active-shooter in your area are greater than you experiencing a terrorist attack or natural disaster. And, if that is not compelling enough, consider that there is nothing more important than protecting our children. What value security if we can't even do that? Any argument?

How have states adapted to include campus/schools as part of homeland security planning?

Many states have permanent campus/school security task forces made up of law enforcement, medical, educators, media, fire service, OEM and others, as part of the state's school and campus security plan. The goal of these task forces is to review best-practices for school and campus security, and to insure that any gaps are discussed and recommendations for mediation brought to the attention of executives and legislators. Regular security exercises at schools including evacuation, lock-downs, active-shooter, fast reporting of emergencies to appropriate authorities, notifications to students, workers, and parents of emergencies, mental health awareness training for students and educators on campus, and training and screening of school bus drivers are just some of the subjects that have been discussed, and protocols established.

How would you go about starting a campus/school security program?

As with other emergencies, just getting the individuals responsible for security of schools and campuses together in one room to get to know each other is 80% of the solution. (And don't forget regional leadership; few politicians will pass up the opportunity.) You would be surprised how many principals and college presidents have never met the Chief of Police or Fire Chief in their area, and *vice versa*. The good ones have.

Prevention of, and preparedness for, disasters is not only about terrorism events.

Chapter 8

Critical Infrastructure Protection

If you enter the words "critical infrastructure protection" in a web search, you will get almost a million hits. Why? One reason is that protecting critical infrastructure is not new; it was a priority even before 9/11. But it was only after 9/11 that people outside of Washington D.C. began focusing on this global security gap. Today, the scope of the effort has expanded, and "cyber-security," "resiliency," and "inter-dependencies" have been added to strategies to protect our critical infrastructure. We'll define these terms in this chapter, but first, let's put the phrase, "critical infrastructure," into simple terms.

One dictionary definition of "infrastructure," and the one that fits here is: *the fundamental facilities and systems serving a country, city, or area, as transportation and communication systems, power plants, and schools.*

Critical infrastructure, then, put in the simplest of terms, are those *places and things that are necessary to sustain and protect life and the way we choose to live it.*

Does that include life-styles, say, sporting events, malls or religious institutions?

While life-styles are not specifically included in the federal list of critical infrastructure sectors (see Fig 6), they are part of the state's responsibility to protect. Any place where people gather in "open environments" (as opposed to a "closed" or controlled venues where all visitors have to be screened, such as airports and government buildings), are possible targets for terrorism and therefore need to be protected (e.g. arenas, stadiums, concert halls, etc.).

Recent History: In May of 1998, President William J. Clinton signed a Presidential Directive (PDD-63) setting up a national program to address the security of our critical infrastructure. Post 9/11, President George W. Bush updated PDD-63 in December 2003 issuing Homeland Security Presidential Directive (HSPD-7) for Critical Infrastructure Identification, Prioritization, and Protection. The directive broadened the definition of infrastructure, as *the physical and virtual systems that are so vital to the United States that the incapacity or destruction of such systems and assets would have a debilitating impact on security, national economic security, national public health or safety*. Europe followed suit with their version in 2006.[15]

The federal response: The Department of Homeland Security (DHS) administers the national programs that protect our critical infrastructure and key resources (CIKR). CIKR is defined by DHS as the assets of the United States essential to the nation's security, public health and safety, economic vitality, and way of life (e.g., energy production and delivery). CIKR is divided into 18 separate sectors, as diverse as agriculture and food, emergency services, and cyber networks.

What role do states play in protecting CIKR?

It is safe to say that administering CIKR protection programs is wholly dependent on having successful partnerships between those responsible for the security and safety of *private sector* and S/L *government agencies*. As previously stated, some states put the CIKR percentage of private sector ownership as high as 90%. That makes "buy-in" from owners and operators to form a partnership with government essential to any measurement of security success. Likewise, relationships between government agencies responsible for security and private sector security agencies are best sustained and nurtured within the communities where these institutions and businesses are located and where their employees are apt to live.

When it comes to risk assessments (see Chapter 4) of individual CIKR facilities, it is the state homeland security resources that facilitate

---

[15]   Directive EU COM 786, European Commission, (2006)

DHS requirements for this information. In turn, the state, through the emergency response community (ERC) insures that the private sector are properly advised of federal and state homeland security activities and information, and that these entities are included in exercises and training on emergency response.

Do these businesses and facilities cooperate?

For the most part, yes. Businesses know that a satisfied employee is more productive, and satisfaction is not just measured in wages and benefits. Safety and security is also important to an employee according to interest groups and unions. Certain companies, such as nuclear power plants, companies using or producing toxic chemicals, and enterprises involved in public transit, have a responsibility to the community and their employees when it comes to safety and security. In some states, CIKR companies and agencies have regular public relations campaigns that involve communities, whether through advertisements or public meetings. In New Jersey, for example, the two nuclear power plants hold bi-annual joint exercises with local responders, and publicize the events. It is the role of the state, however, though the governor's office and respective homeland security advisors to maintain close relationships with CIKR facilities and agencies, and encourage transparent security and safety practices when possible. It is simply good business practice.

Can you be more specific on what types of facilities make up CIKR?

If you're looking for specific listings with sectors, sub-sectors, segments and sub-segments of CIKR, please refer to the DHS website and search under "CIKR Information Data Taxonomy." Having people agree with definitions of what comprises, say, a nuclear "facility," "site," or "plant," is virtually impossible. Still, DHS is more than happy to try to explain it to you. Frankly, unless you have a legal need, you don't need to go there.

That said, a definition of CIKR bears repeating:

Critical Infrastructure (CI) are the assets, systems, and networks, whether physical or virtual, so vital to the United States that their incapacitation or destruction would have a debilitating effect on security, national economic security, public health or safety, or any combination thereof.

Key Resources (KR) are publicly or privately controlled resources essential to the minimal operations of the economy and government.

Fig. 5 CIKR Def.

The National Infrastructure Protection Plan (NIPP) is quite specific about what comprises the CIKR sectors. According to the 2009 NIPP,[16] they are as follows:

Agriculture and Food	Banking and Finance	Chemical
Commercial Facilities	Communications	Critical Manufacturing
Dams	Defense Industrial Base	Emergency Services
Energy	Government Facilities	Healthcare and Public Health
Information Technology	National Monuments and Icons	Nuclear Reactors, Materials & Waste
Postal and Shipping	Transportation Systems	Water

Fig. 6 CIKR Sectors

---

[16] *Ad ibid*

What about cyber infrastructure?

Although not specified as a "sector," it is significant to note that all eighteen of the above sectors rely heavily on computers and cyberspace in their operations. That is one reason why securing our <u>cyber</u> assets has become more of a concern. There have been increased cyber-attacks against both private and government facilities, especially our military and energy plants. A meltdown of a cyber-system maintaining, say, energy, health, finance, or defense sectors would significantly cripple their ability to function. The threat is both *technical*, that is, improper and insufficient "firewall" protection of computers, and *human*, businesses not all requiring background checks of system employees, or an impromptu attack by a disgruntled systems administrator.

The threat of cyber-terrorism and cyber-crime, as well as disruptive "hackers," has prompted the federal government to mount an awareness and operational campaign to counter the danger. In December 2009, President Barak Obama named a new Cyber Security Coordinator, Howard A. Schmidt, to lead the effort to shore up the country's computer networks and better coordinate with companies that operate 80% of those critical systems. In 2010, the president put the federal response to cyber security under DHS. The National Cyberspace Response System oversees risk-assessments and response to attacks, and is led by DHS' National Cyber Security Division (NCSD). Federal Cyber-Security Conferences, public congressional hearings and interaction with private entities have proliferated, and the trend will continue, especially since it is a dynamic discipline. DHS statistics between 2006 and 2008, reflect a 300% increase in cyber-attacks against sectors and another uptick in 2010 and 2011.

Some states have joined up regionally to promote cyber-security awareness among public and private entities. Several states have sponsored Cyber-Security workshops and conferences as well as developed state equivalents of the U.S. Computer Emergency Response Teams (U.S. CERTs).

What is meant by "resiliency" and "interdependence" among CIKRs?

Resiliency—Interesting choice of word, because infrastructure cannot return to its original state, as when new, or recover from damage on its own, as the literal definition would imply. However, "resiliency" has become a "buzz" word in the homeland security lexicon, so we are stuck with it. We recommend you think of "strengthening and fortifying our infrastructure," when you hear the word "resiliency" used in this context.

The point is that without a plan to rebuild, refurbish, and constantly maintain the "bricks and mortar" of infrastructure, it will eventually crumble. So, any plan to protect our critical infrastructure, sector by sector, has to examine and require attention to "resiliency."

As previously mentioned, the 2009 NIPP has emphasized "resiliency" as part of CIKR protection assessments. The reason is because experts have been warning about overlooking resiliency as part of a homeland security and preparedness strategy for some time. Two examples of published studies underlining this recommendation are: George Mason University School of Law's 2007, Critical Thinking: Moving from Infrastructure Protection to Infrastructure Resilience[17], and Stephen Flynn's book, The Edge of Disaster: Rebuilding a Resilient Nation.[18]

Our critical infrastructure is "crumbling?"

The adjective is for effect, but yes, bridges, levies, tunnels, dikes, dams, roads, nuclear reactors, etc., all have a finite "shelf-life." Much of the nation's infrastructure was built at the turn of the last century, and another build followed WWII. Since then, no serious investments have been made to shore up the nation's infrastructure, even though roads, tunnels, bridges, levies, etc., were only predicted to last 50 years or so

---

[17] Critical Thinking: Moving from Infrastructure Protection to Infrastructure Resilience, George Mason University, School of Law, Critical Infrastructure Protection Program, Discussion Studies Series, February 2007

[18] The Edge of Disaster: Rebuilding a Resilient Nation, Flynn, Stephen E., Random House Inc., New York, 2007.

when built. The best we have been able to do (read: afford) is patch, patch, patch. Meanwhile, traffic and use of the nation's infrastructure has increased dramatically over the years, and, again according to the experts, patching will not hold up for long.

Why haven't we done more to fix this problem?

The main reason that we have not dropped what we are doing and pitched in to reverse this erosion, is the politically unpalatable cost associated with each project. The rebuilding or refurbishing of current "fossils" will run in the billions of dollars per state, some say it is a trillion dollar national enterprise—not a very attractive political issue to take on. It is more memorable for a politician to invest in building more schools in his or her district than to take on fixing, say, a waterway levy effecting his or her district that the U.S. Army Corp of Engineers predicts is apt to fail at any moment. Meanwhile, experts are screaming that we have no choice; we cannot afford NOT to shore up our CIKR.

While it may sound like "fear-mongering" to some, the facts as laid out by both George Mason University and Dr. Flynn are compelling and logical. And, unlike other controversial issues, such as global warming, there is no point and counter-point; no one disagrees about the threat posed by our aging infrastructure.

The good news is that, nationally, leaders are starting to come around. Funds from the stimulus package are programmed for rebuild the most needy CIKR. Another step was taken when DHS added "resilience" to "preparedness and protection" on the homeland security public policy agenda. As DHS points out, however, implementation of this policy will require serious investments by federal and state governments, as well as the private sector. So far, we are only in the nascent stage; proposals are still lagging behind other "priority" investments. Hopefully, it will not take another bridge collapse, as recently occurred in Minneapolis, MN, before more urgency is placed on the issue.

Interdependencies—The reference is to the <u>interaction</u> between critical infrastructure sectors during disasters or major emergencies. Think: "interconnected" and "mutually dependent."

We referenced earlier in this chapter how cyberspace linked all 18 CIKR, how an attack on the cyber system can disrupt hospitals, energy, finance, etc. During certain disasters, hurricanes for example, evacuation of a densely populated area requires that transportation services be alerted, that petroleum companies activate key gasoline stations along evacuation routes, that emergency response agencies open reverse lanes for these services—one sector dependent on the others. And while some disasters do not require evacuations, interdependence of the various sectors is still required. A dam failure in one region can affect crop production and sanitation services down the line. In urban areas, life support systems are interdependent because of their physical proximity and operational interaction. Say a cast-iron water main ruptures in a major city where much of the infrastructure is underground. The damage would extend to electrical systems, communications cables and gas mains with system-wide consequences.

For these reasons, most national and regional conferences dealing with critical infrastructure protection will, for the foreseeable future, include "resilience" and "interdependencies" as main parts of discussions. For these reasons, the context of these words needs to be understood from grade school level up.

Chapter 9

Grants Programs

Anyone who has worked for a state, local, tribal or territorial government agency knows that budgets, even in the wealthier regions that have strong tax bases, are notoriously limited and meticulously scrutinized, especially when items involve public safety prevention programs. *Real* threats, such as drugs, gangs and violence, take precedence over *possible* threats such as those posed by terrorism and natural disasters.

After 9/11, great demands were placed on S/L emergency agencies to prepare for an "imminent" next attack. (You'll recall the experts and politicians quoting, "It is not a question of if, but when.") Fittingly, the federal government recognized the limitation of S/L budgets and through DHS' S*tate, Local and Tribal Grant Programs,* began distributing grant funds, especially in high-risk areas. Congress quickly obliged Administration requests for funding and a windfall rained down on unprepared S/L agencies. The dash-for-the-cash was on.

State, Local and Tribal Grant Programs (SLTGP), which were zero in 2001, hit a high of almost 4 billion dollars in 2006. Since then they stabilized to just over $2B for fiscal year 2010 and then started dropping. The FY 2012 budget was cut to $1.3B. Accordingly, and DHS through FEMA, its grant management agency, has started to apply strict sustainability and risk-based requirements to its 17 individual SLTGPs, which fall into three groupings: Homeland Security Grants, Preparedness Grants (formerly Infrastructure Protection Programs), and Other Grants (see Figure 6). In 2012, these grant programs were reduced to nine.

Homeland Security Grants	Preparedness Grants	Other Grants
State Homeland Security	Transit Security Grant Program	Tribal Homeland Security Grant Program
Urban Area Security Initiative Grant	Intercity Passenger Rail Program	Nonprofit Security Grant Program
Operation Stonegarden	Port Security Grant Program	Emergency Management Performance Grants

Figure 6 SLTGP

It is safe to say that federal assistance in the form of grant funding will be around for some time but the funding continues to be reduced. After all, the threat of international terrorism and natural disasters are national concerns and well beyond the ability of even the largest and wealthiest regions of the country to adequately fund. That said, states have to be judicious in their long-term planning when applying for these federal grants. National priorities can shift unexpectedly and the economic imbalance we are facing may persist. For these reasons, it has been the "rule of thumb" for some time that S/Ls should view federal assistance as "seed money" for needed programs. For one thing, that approach is more palatable to Congress and Administration grant managers because it underscores the sustainable quality of the investments.

What do you mean by "Seed Money?"

It refers to using grant funding to *initiate* a needed program or capability rather than absorbing the funding into a re-occurring expense cycle. The classic example of poor planning of grant funds is using funding to supplement salaries of full-time employees. In those cases, the question you need ask is: When the funding dries up, can your budget afford to keep them? Another example is the municipality that requests funding for, say, an emergency command truck, but doesn't have the local maintenance budget to sustain it. Or using federal dollars to buy a helicopter to start an aerial surveillance program, when they should know that the cheapest part of such an endeavor is the price of the aircraft; funding the salary for the pilots, parts, storage, and mechanics will have to be paid with local funds.

In other words, think sustainability. In turn, if your grant application addresses how you are going to cover maintenance and management costs in the following years, it stands a better chance of getting approved.

How else does DHS rate effective grant programs?

Besides "sustainability," DHS (FEMA) requires that grant programs to be "risk-based." State Administrative Agents (SAAs), the states' designated managers of grant funding to each state, need to insure that applications are in line with national as well as regional priorities. State vulnerability assessments for the 18 CIKR sectors, for example, should reflect the priorities of the investment applications. Recently, DHS has emphasized states identifying capability gaps then steering investments to fill those gaps. How many gaps and how well they are progressing are also measures of effectiveness. But the bottom line test for effectiveness is for the state to be able to articulate at some point *how well these investments have bought down risk* in their area.

How can a state control abuse of grant funding?

Abuse, whether in the form of "favoritism" or just plain mismanagement, can be controlled, at least in great part by the state issuing clear guidelines to applicants about criteria, and then applying strict auditing and accounting practices. An example of clear criteria for an application is to instruct planners that all investments should:

1. Follow a risk-based system
2. Significantly benefit the state's emergency response community
3. Support the national and state priorities, and target capabilities, e.g., interoperability, regionalization, and information sharing
4. Avoid duplication

Another way to defer abuse and criticism of favoritism is for the state to de-centralize the approval process of applications. The SAA can form stakeholder committees to review and recommend applications, per the above criteria, before being submitted to the SAA. The stakeholders for the Urban Area Security Initiative (UASI), for example, are those agencies eligible to receive grant funding for that program. Likewise, for the Preparedness Grant programs, representatives of the 18 CIKR sectors are the stakeholders. Rather than fielding information and applications direct, an SAA can refer potential applicants to the appropriate committee.

This management practice incorporates the best practices outlined in Chapter 2 (Interagency Coordination), Chapter 4 (Risk-based Management), and Chapter 5 (Private/Public Partnerships). Applied together, they leave little to criticize.

Chapter 10

Catastrophic Events Planning

Catastrophic events, often called **mega-disasters,** are of such severe consequences that their effects cut across public and private sectors, damaging life, property and the psyche of the nation. In fact, it is safe to say that most are difficult to comprehend and are nothing like what you see in movies, although with the latest technical animations, some come close.

Examples of what can be called a catastrophic event are pandemics and nuclear explosions, as well as certain hurricanes, earthquakes, tsunamis, cyber and other terrorist attacks whose intensity cross beyond the capability to recover without a national or international response. In some cases, rehabilitation is extremely difficult, and takes one or more generations, e.g., Pompeii and Hiroshima. In that regard, most natural emergencies, accidents and even terrorist attacks do not meet the criteria of a catastrophic event. Think: 1) severe consequences that exhaust state emergency capabilities to respond and recover, 2) national in scope, 3) traumatic casualties both physical and mental, and 4) life and life style-altering.

In the end, the definition or designation of a catastrophic event is modified to fit the circumstances. Academically, it can be argued, for example, that the 9/11 attacks or the Oklahoma City bombing were not "catastrophic" in and of themselves. However, add to the event the awakening of the consciousness of a nation and other consequences, and the argument can tilt in the other direction. Katrina and the 2010 earthquakes in Haiti and Chili, however, are clearly catastrophic, the magnitude of which leave in doubt whether those areas can or cannot totally recover.

Theoretically, state emergency response-planning for catastrophic events, whether natural or man-made, is similar to federal strategies, except that the focus of the state is more on preparedness rather than prevention. Prevention of catastrophic terrorist events, such as a paralyzing and coordinated cyber-attack on CIKRs or a nuclear detonation in the homeland rests primarily with the federal government. But as we have said before, all emergencies begin local and so preparedness for such events still involves the states. Concomitantly, the federal government is required to support the state preparedness effort; in fact, most states will not plan for catastrophic events without federal support and funding.

What are the main impediments to state preparedness planning?

The main impediment is one we have discussed before, a degree of complacency (read priority) on the part of states, counties, territories, or municipalities to engage in vigorous planning programs. In most jurisdictions, public funds are already stretched beyond limits fighting local security emergencies such as drugs, gangs, and violence. "Do I vote to fund more neighborhood watch and school security programs?" asks the stressed Mayor of a violence-plagued city, "Or push to fund catastrophic disaster preparedness training?" i.e., an on-going emergency, versus, a probable one. The answer, if that is the only choice she or he has, is a no-brainer.

The fact that state catastrophic event-planning *has* to be subsidized by federal grants makes it essential that state emergency planners work closely with FEMA, and agree on a strategy that best fits their needs. Utilizing regionalization (working with neighboring emergency responders) on mega-disaster preparedness training exercises just makes sense. After all, it will be these interagency and inter-state agencies that will be called upon to respond in a coordinated fashion during, and following, a catastrophic event. Recently, FEMA has made it clear that it strongly supports this leadership and coordination from state' agencies so that it will be there when the time comes.

Do all mega-disasters have a similar basic "catastrophic" response plan?

From a public health and emergency life-saving point of view, response by medical and HazMat responders is similar in approach. A mass-casualty event, whether burns, poison, or traumatic injuries, will need similar staging, such as battlefield *"triage"* and field medical treatment or decontamination centers. But when it comes to other factors such as addressing mega-disaster command and control (who is in charge and what are the protocols to follow?) and efforts to mitigate damage and engage the public with necessary information, different events will have different planning requirements.

Remember that the emergency objective of the responder who arrives at the scene first is to keep the emergency from getting worse, even before seeing to the sick and injured. Upon learning of a reported explosion, for example, the first question by responders has to be, "which way is the wind blowing?" (in order to establish a proper on-scene command post) The second is containment. These questions or reactions will vary during, say, a pending hurricane, where you have more time to prepare the response.

When it comes to responding to a catastrophic event, the only constant is the reaction of the local emergency response community (ERC), whose experience usually lies in the series of daily and relatively minor crises management situations. Unfortunately, preparedness for a catastrophic event has to recognize that there will not be enough local response capability no matter how well trained and equipped the responders are; morbidity and mortality will abound.

A *basic* preparedness plan for catastrophic events, therefore, must at least contain a realistic understanding of these consequences. For example, you can count on the fact that someone has to step up; there will be a hunger for leadership among the population, as was the case during Katrina.

However, most experts agree that in the end, it will be the logical and personal judgment of individuals and small groups of individuals that will save the day and avoid the mass casualties of a mega disaster. Preparedness is the key, but absent that, it will be the resilience of the population and the will to survive that will make the difference.

a) **Bioterrorism**—Simply put, the definition of bio-type terrorism is: the intentional release or dissemination of biological agents such as bacteria, viruses, toxins or other germs (agents) used to cause illness or death in people, animals, or plants.

The federal government's Center for Disease Control and Prevention (CDC) points out that *these agents are typically found in nature, but it is possible that they could be changed to increase their ability to cause disease, make them resistant to current medicines, or to increase their ability to be spread into the environment. Biological agents can be spread through the air, through water, or in food. They are difficult to detect and reaction to them is not immediate, sometimes hours or days. Some bioterrorism agents, like the smallpox virus, can be spread from person to person and some, like anthrax, cannot.*[19] Thus, response plans will be slow to evolve, and prevention of further illness requires a coherent plan of communication, and good information. <u>A personal plan is necessary</u>.

Considerable information is available through the CDC on this subject including other indicators, reactions, prevention programs and response. You can research the subject at http://www.bt.cdc.gov/bioterrorism/.

b) **Chemical-Terrorism**—Chemical-type terrorism is related to bio-type (natural) agents, and is comprised of those agents that are formed by chemical components or a combination of them. And while biological agents

---

[19] <u>Bioterrorim Overview</u>, Centers for Disease Control and Prevention, 2008-02-12, retrieved 2009-05-22.

have to be released covertly (unnatural for someone to legally possess anthrax), chemical agents can be used more overtly (rat poison in a food supply). In both cases, however, the state ERC needs to keep in mind that in preparing for this type of terrorism a broader group of experts have to be engaged, especially from the academic (scientific) community and related government agencies.

There are hundreds of chemicals that are toxic. They are broken down in four agency groups, <u>Cyanide</u>, <u>Pulmonary</u>, <u>Vesicants/Blistering</u>, and <u>Nerve</u>. The ones most recognized by the public are arsenic, ammonia, caustic acids, chlorine, cyanide, tear gas, and toxic alcohols.

These toxins can be released in the air or in the water and will have almost immediate effects, and require good information quickly to prevent further casualties. State and federal homeland security, health care and CDC websites have preventative and emergency information on the subject. Each person should have some basic knowledge to develop a personal response. Keep in mind that should a suspected event occur, the best response may not be evacuation—sheltering in place may actually work best.

State preparedness programs should integrate training and research on the five focus areas CDC uses in their strategic plan for chemical as well as biological threats:

- ✓ Preparedness and Prevention
- ✓ Detection and Surveillance
- ✓ Diagnosis and characterization of chemical and biological agents
- ✓ Response
- ✓ Communications

c) **Nuclear Event and the "Dirty Bomb"**—Radiological Dispersal Devises (RDDs) are the most dramatic terrorist tactic. Note: we do not refer to it as the most destructive.

Preparing for the possibility of an RDD terrorist attack, states should focus on a similar strategy as noted above with bio and chemical terrorism. However, the use of an RDD on the homeland will also cause traumatic consequences, and thought must be given to educating the public on how to react to such an event. The lessons of yesteryear (remember the Civil Defense exercises?) are for the most part applicable for RDDs and state planners should "dust off" those manuals for applicable parts, and place them on convenient Web locations. For example, the public should know to seek underground refuge after a close-by nuclear event instead of trying to flee the area.

When it comes to the threat of RDDs, most of the attention has to be on preventing (detecting) a plot before it manifests itself. And, most of that prevention effort is in the hands of the federal government. Still, there is much a state can do in support of detecting a nuclear terrorist plot, including training and exercising on detection equipment and a clear understanding of the effects and limitations of a RDD.

So what *is* a "dirty bomb?"

RDDs fall into two main categories: *nuclear bombs* of different magnitude (measured by the equivalent of the effect of tons of TNT, e.g., the bomb dropped on Hiroshima was the equivalent of 10-megatons of TNT going off at once and on one location. A *"dirty bomb,"* which is a conventional bomb containing radiological "debris," such as radiological waste from hospitals and universities. The main difference between the two is the amount of radiological "fallout." A "dirty bomb" will set off detectors the same way a nuclear bomb would but when detonated will not have the same radiological intensity and killing-power from radiation.

States, especially in densely populated areas, have to discuss the response and effects of both. This priority has not manifested itself among most states, since, as we discussed earlier, it falls in the mega-disaster syndrome of competing priorities and the rationale that "it just won't happen here." But if a nuclear event does occur, there is little anyone can do to help the initial wave of victims. Emergency Medical Services (EMS) will be unable to reach the areas of highest radiation. The first order of business will be to define the areas where survivors are most likely to be. Personal training is essential since EMS and others may not reach survivors for weeks.

d) **Cyber-terrorism**—As we pointed out earlier, one of the most crippling terrorist scenarios, involves a coordinated cyber-attack. Cyber-systems have become the "backbones" of most CIKR operations. According to DHS, between 2006 and 2008, cyber-attacks have tripled in number, from over 20,000 to over 60,000 by sector. On April 8, 2009, the Wall Street Journal reported that "Cyber spies have penetrated the U.S. electrical grid and left behind software programs that could be used to disrupt the system, according to current and former national security officials."

Defending these cyber systems falls on each entity to develop, maintain, and update. The sharing of specific technology to protect individual systems (public and private) is not practical because of the proprietary nature of tailored systems. However, partnerships to discuss general technical solutions or threat statuses are not only practical but necessary. The federal government has concluded that our main defense against cyber-attacks is the steady exchange of ideas and information by those charged with protecting these systems, sector by sector.

States have to insure that any partnership or information sharing includes a discussion of the human factor related to cyber-terrorism. The enemy knows that while U.S. protection technology is advanced, the use of a human penetration is a viable option where companies and agencies are lax with background checks for those individuals responsible for protecting cyber systems. It is common practice by U.S. enemies to exploit the disgruntled or greedy employee. Other countries have experienced this type of havoc. In 2000, a disgruntled employee rigged a computerized control system at a water-treatment plant in Australia, releasing more than 200,000 gallons of sewage into parks, rivers, and the grounds of a Hyatt hotel. Hardly a mega-disaster, but exemplary of a resource that can be exploited for, say, a coordinated multi-sector attack. All the technical fire-walls in the universe cannot defeat that type of attack.

Chapter 11

Public Awareness

As a general rule, the public is not interested in disaster planning or preparedness. While that might sound harsh, the truth is that disasters are "low probability" events, and so are not able to compete for attention with the priorities of daily life. Examples abound that attest to the public's illogical apathy or complacency, including the shore population of hurricane-prone areas (30% would not leave when ordered to do so), or those along "tornado alley" in the mid-west (93% do not have underground shelters), or those living along earthquake fault lines ("tremors just go with the territory.")

A major challenge in preparedness efforts then is for planners to try to maintain a sane level of focus among the elected officials, organizational leaders, businesses, and the public in general on the potential consequences of disasters, and how to react to them. Before this challenge can be addressed, however, the main obstacles must be examined. For example, an inter-governmental paradox exists in disaster planning: because considerable federal support and involvement follows large disasters, there is a standing public perception that major disasters will be automatically and appropriately handled by the federal government. When in fact, the brunt of life-saving measures will rely on volunteers (those who are still able, that is) to help local first responders and others in the community. Federal and state assistance may be days or weeks away, or, as in the case of a nationwide pandemic or local "dirty bomb," perhaps not at all.

Many emergency planners and visionaries are advocating more awareness and engagement by the public in the same way that Civil Defense measures of the 1950s and '60s brought attention into schools, workplaces, and homes. No one argues with the old adage that "an ounce of prevention is worth more than a pound of cure." The trick is how to sell it without getting plummeted with accusations of "fear-mongering."

Many seminars and workshops have been held towards *understanding* public apathy, which is the first step towards planning for it. According to FEMA, public apathy stems mainly from:

- ✓ **Lack of Awareness**
- ✓ **Underestimation of Risk**
- ✓ **Reliance on Technology**
- ✓ **Fatalism/Denial**
- ✓ **Social Pressures**[20]

Nowhere in these studies, however, has the notion of elementary school education, for example, or any type of public education for that matter, mentioned as part of a solution. At the very least, a steady flow of public awareness campaigns, a provocative iterative process, has to be a key part of emergency planning, and especially for major disasters. Think of what "Smokey Bear" ads have done to prevent forest fires. That campaign was a logical extension of mom and dad admonishing children not to play with matches.

A state commitment to educate K-12 students needs to start with the will of state leadership to engage in such a campaign. In high risk areas, the effort is more palatable, but obstacles can be anticipated, both from parents and teachers. Still, it is a debate worth having if we are going to be serious about homeland security and an effective preparedness effort.

Does the media have a role?

The media are stakeholders in a comprehensive campaign. Since a well-informed public will usually make proper decisions, the news

---

[20] Disaster Response: Principles of Preparation and Coordination, Adapted from Auf derHeide. 1989. St. Louis, Missouri: C.V. Mosby and Company, pp. 14-17.

media has to be on the top of the list of worthy allies. Most state agencies have public information officers (PIOs) and protocols about who, when and how public information is dispersed. Warning: homeland security information cannot be "spun" politically by PIOs—the public is unforgiving when it feels it is being lied to, and doing so is counterproductive.

Obviously, the state needs to speak with one authoritative voice on issues, especially public safety and security—public confidence being key to public acceptance of information. Government must demonstrate to the public its leadership through programs of education and accountability. The media, when a mutually-respectful working partnership has been formed, can be a formidable government ally in keeping the public properly informed.

Obviously, there are times when inside information has to be protected, as is the case during ongoing investigations or when dealing with confidential sources of the intelligence community. But for the most part, the media understands and respects these caveats. PIOs earn their keep maintaining a balanced flow of information so that the public does not feel it is on the "bottom of the food chain"—least we forget, it is the public who pays their salaries.

Towards this end, state homeland security advisors should sponsor and encourage PIO workshops on how emergency information should be handled under different situations. Establishing and exercising a joint information center (JIC) at emergency operations centers for when the time comes is a way of bringing PIOs together, establishing disaster info protocols, and centralizing messaging to the public. That process is an effective part of pre-planning for major emergencies.

What other techniques can state governments use to keep the public engaged?

Another practical pro-active approach is to capitalize on "slow" news days. Often, the media will look to promote public awareness messages during those times. Because the subject of homeland security resonates with the public, especially the topics of "terrorism" and "emergency response," a PIO can usually find a receptive audience and take advantage of media availability.

Also, when a natural or man-made disaster occurs anywhere around the globe, state homeland security advisors can use the opportunity to engage the public in a dialogue either through the media or by staging a workshop or conference to discuss the consequences of such an event happening within their state or community. A timely provocative discussion initiated by the state on a relevant subject will often defeat the nay-sayers and pundits who are quick to play the "blame-game" and criticize others for "what went wrong."

There are other tactics the state can practice to engage the public. Civic groups, industry, faith-based institutions, schools and centers of higher learning are always looking for speakers for their public or private gatherings. Get your spokesperson on a public speaking forum. The subject of homeland security is compelling, and a steady investment in these local engagements will pay dividends during emergencies.

In other words, when it comes to public information, stay current, relevant and engaged.

I thought emergency responders were taught to avoid the media?

The emergency response community and other public servants are not automatic spokespersons for their agency or the state. That is the role of PIOs, specialists who know the protocols, policies, networking and vetting rules by which information can and should be released to the public. Information that can compromise an operation, for example, is embargoed for obvious reasons. Any proactive outreach to the media and the public must be part of emergency planning and properly exercised. Remember, inaccurate or poorly timed information is not only counter-productive, it might endanger lives.

That said, engaging the public, even if it's to tell them that the state is working on a problem and to be patient, is good business. The public has a right to know that public servants are on top of situation and will keep them appropriately informed.

Have you ever been to a dentist who does not keep you informed as to what he or she is doing and why? Very frightening.

Chapter 12

Legal Issues

Activities on homeland security were born out of necessity. In the years that immediately followed 9/11, lawmakers and policymakers quickly assembled strategies and a body of laws authorizing and empowering federal and state agencies to better protect the homeland from a ruthless and relentless foreign enemy. As with all new laws, adjustments are often necessary and a new legal specialty emerged: *homeland security law*.

On the federal side, traditional legal responsibilities such as immigration, maritime, customs, trade and environment needed to be bolstered, and changes were administered primarily by the new department that in 2003 merged 22 security and emergency response agencies: The Department of Homeland Security (DHS).

Federal and state legislation added statutory rules and regulations governing such things as environment, best-business-practices, administration, civil liberties, auditing and other policies that are also binding on certain public agencies as well as industry. Of course, laws and legal opinions are subject to interpretation, thus a new specialty within the practice of law quickly emerged.

Consider: DHS alone has over 1700 attorneys, 800 of which are devoted to just Immigration.

So there were no homeland security laws before 9/11?

Yes, there were. It is worth noting that this body of work (homeland security and all its aspects) was not created out of "whole cloth." Most of the 9/11 Commission recommendations,[21] for example, were built on foundations laid by previously established emergency preparedness rules and standards, such as the American National Standard on Disaster/Emergency Management and Business Continuity Programs, also known as the National Fire Protection Association Standard 1600 (NFPA 1600). (The current version of NFPA 1600 is available on the Internet at: http://www.nfpa.org/assets/files/pdf/nfpa1600.pdf.)

Post 9/11 security legislation and policies were aimed primarily at *enhancing* existing government procedures and *encouraging* the private sector to implement standards and emergency plans for operations, response, recovery, and continuity for their institutions. The Patriot Act is an example of "enhancing" government procedures by lowering the legal requirements needed to obtain court-ordered electronic surveillance against suspected terrorists (see Chapter 6). Requiring industries that use or manufacture dangerous toxins to initiate research on "inherently safer technology," is an example of "encouraging" the private sector. The intent is to bring the private sector into line with the national plan, especially since 80-90% of potential terrorist targets are controlled by the private sector (see Chapter 8).

What about all this reforming of immigration laws?

While immigration laws (enforcement, adjudications, and service) are controlled by DHS and aimed, among other things, at securing our borders, S/L communities are often directly affected by shoddy enforcement and service. Whatever the related issue, all seem to agree that new migration policy, and by extension—legislation, is needed. The White House has indicated it is in favor of reviving a major overhaul discussion with Congress[22]. The main issue revolves around what do to with the estimated 10.8 million (and counting) illegal immigrants in the U.S.—Amnesty? Arrest and deport?

---

[21]   Ibid, pg. 14
[22]   Obama looking to give new life to Immigration Reform, March 4, 2010, Los Angeles Times, Peter Nicholas

It is a complicated issue and action to address it has been slow. The reason is that immigration reform is a daunting enterprise that cuts across the social and economic fabric of the nation—a fabric that is beginning to look more like a patchwork quilt of mini-reforms. For example, revised visa application process, new Passport requirements, time-consuming background check, work-screening programs, and stiffer border entry procedures are but a few of the recent adjustments to immigration security procedures, and more are anticipated. Meanwhile, some point to the loss of tourism-related revenue, which has dropped by 17% during recent years, although analysts also blame the global economic down-turn.

Doesn't all of this illegal immigration make localities less safe?

The point is that the jury is still out as to whether the country is "safer" as a result of these enhancements. Abuses, on both sides of the issue, are unavoidable. Logic says that condoning an illegal activity is debilitating. Just look at the illegal substance laws we choose to ignore. It also drains the morale of law enforcement, which is caught in the middle. Obviously, finding a legal way to absorb the millions of undocumented workers will help law enforcement in the "sorting" process aimed at uncovering criminals and terrorists that threaten our security. The inability to "sort," leads to "profiling" tactics, or non-compliance with their sworn duties.

The legal give-and-take over "security at the expense of civil liberties" will no doubt continue as long as foreign terrorists insist on killing Americans and our way of life. And, every terrorist act committed in this country exacerbates the debate. In this regard, "it is inevitable," says Gus P. Coldebella, former General Counsel for DHS, "that lawyers will need to assist businesses in the Patriot Act, Homeland Security Act as well as recent regulations and statutory procedures that affect all industries, not only critical infrastructure."[23]

---

[23]   Is the United States Safer from a Terrorist Attack Today than before Sept.11?, An interview with Michael Chertoff and Gus Coldebella, New Jersey Lawyer Magazine, October 2007, No. 248

Is it true then that most homeland security legal issues have a federal focus?

Most controversial legal issues involving homeland security, the ones you are apt to see on the 6 o'clock news, such as immigration reform, border security, Patriot Act related actions—electronic surveillance, arrest and prosecution of terrorists, are certainly in the federal domain. However, these actions spill over into state jurisdictions and communities.

Some states have established a cabinet-level Public Advocate Office to review any civil rights considerations related to state homeland security policies, procedures or litigation. State Chief Counsels and Attorneys General also play an oversight role in state "prevention" operations and other legal considerations, such as terrorist-related state prosecutions, state Emergency Declarations, ethics violations, and auditing of homeland security budgets and grants.

Are terrorists prosecuted by the individual states?

Most states have penal codes and statutes making acts of terrorism a specific crime when committed within the respective state. However, by individual agreements between the state Attorneys General and the respective United States Attorney for the federal district, terrorists and terrorism-related offenses are prosecuted as federal crimes.

What about Tribunals and Enemy Combatants?

Traditionally, the term "enemy combatant" refers to captured member of the armed forces of an enemy state. A military Tribunal is usually established to determine whether a captive is an enemy combatant subject to the terms of the Geneva Convention. However, neither members of Al Qaeda, the Taliban or their affiliates and sympathizers are members of "armed forces of a state" and so any captive in these organizations falls under the designation of "illegal combatant." The detainees at Guantanamo, for example, fall under this category. Military tribunals have been set up to determine the status of these detainees, and therein lies some of the confusion.

The states are not involved in this process directly. Occasionally, members of a state's National Guard, who have been federalized (called up for the wars in Iraq and Afghanistan), are subpoenaed to testify at military tribunals, but that involvement is related to the federal process.

What is the role of District Attorneys or County Prosecutors in homeland security?

Each state is broken down into districts, which usually follow county boundaries. Within each district or county, there is a criminal prosecutor, sometimes called District Attorney, Country Prosecutor or State's Prosecutor. Since most states' homeland security prevention strategies operate under an all-crimes/all-hazards paradigm, these county prosecutors play a key role in prioritizing police actions and information-sharing plans.

Within the law enforcement hierarchy, criminal prosecutions are under the control of county prosecutors, who in turn follow the guidelines established by the "top-cop" in the state, the state Attorney General. In terrorism-related investigations, the collaboration between respective United States Attorney Offices and State Attorneys General and County Prosecutors, is key, and should parallel operational relationships between federal and state investigators. (See Chapter 6, Section d, Joint Terrorism Task Forces)

Has 9/11 changed the state's approach to interrogations of suspected terrorists?

No, and it is unlikely that the issue of "enhanced interrogation techniques," a euphemism for "torture," is apt to come up at a state-level prosecution. All law enforcement officials are "sworn" personnel, which means they are sworn to uphold the Constitution of the United States as well as the constitution of the respective state. Under the law, when an investigation focuses on an individual, and when that individual is confronted by a law enforcement official, the law enforcement official is required to advise the person of his or her rights to remain silent and to have a defense attorney present during any questioning. The individual also has to be informed that anything he or she says can, and will, be used against them in a court of law, that a court attorney can be provided before any questioning, and that they can terminate the questioning at any time. The individual then has to acknowledge a clear understanding of those rights and waive them, before he or she can be questioned. So ingrained is this requirement of law enforcement, known as the Miranda warning, that most law enforcement officials know it by rote and even video tape and require witnesses as part of the procedures. The issue of "torture," therefore, is so far beyond conventional law enforcement techniques to render the possibility moot.

Are homeland security legal issues increasing or leveling out?

It is safe to say, that legal issues are increasing in the field of homeland security. For one thing, the discipline is dynamic, that is, constantly changing. For another, the enemy is relentless and our interests continue to be global. As a result, experts are predicting more terrorism attacks on the homeland. If that were to happen, the legal debate over "security at the expense of civil rights" will take center stage again.

At the same time, border security and violence are escalating, and natural disaster experts are predicting less, albeit more fierce, natural disasters. Security technology also continues to evolve and tools such as biometric human identification, radio-frequency identification, and body-scanners carry "intrusiveness," and "business-altering" legal issues. Port and chemical security regulations and rules are also the subject of legal scrutiny because of uncertain costs related to changes in established international treaties[24] and industry rules, such as governing the development of inherently safer technology and protection of CIKR, need constant interpretation.

Government rules and mandates are always controversial because of associated cost factors and the perception of intrusiveness.

---

[24]   International Ship and Port Facility Security Code, amendment to the Safety of Life at Sea (SOLAS) Convention (1974/1988), London July 1, 2004

What happens to the rule of law(s) during and after a catastrophe?

That question is a fitting end to this overview. Some say history is prologue, and if that is true, the lessons learned from Katrina are poignant. As previously mentioned, keeping the emergency from escalating is the first order of business during a crises. Nothing will exacerbate a crisis more than lawlessness. Yet, we see the signs time and time again during disasters—"looters will be shot"—The antithesis of law and order.

Lawyers are needed to prepare the emergency response community in crisis-management law and ethical behavior. Legal issues should always be a component of all emergency exercises. Lawyers will also be in high demand following the disaster to assess, evaluate, mitigate and advise.

Where lawmakers have been used wisely to prepare for emergencies, the area has been more secure. During the disaster, however, when public services are overwhelmed, it will be the public itself who will determine lawful behavior and will need to police itself.

That said, legal interpretations (read, Homeland Security Law) will be around for some time to come.

Acknowledgments

On such a diverse and complicated subject, no one person can claim credit or expertise on all the components that make up state homeland security. A group of people, much more talented than I, offered their advice and support in compiling this primer and they deserve recognition.

I specifically want to thank Dr. Paul Lioy from Rutgers University, not only for his intellectual prowess but for his friendship during the editing . . . editing . . . and more editing. Eric and Jeff Kutner brought a blend of academic study and real-world practice that is unique and an effective combination. (They even convinced their talented mother, Nancy Kutner, to contribute to the editing.) My fellow former homeland security advisors from Virginia, Bob Crouch, and from Maryland, Dennis Schrader, also provided input, advice and encouragement, as well as the respected Ed Willever, the quintessential emergency responder. A "tip of the hat" also goes to Tom Moran, the Executive Director for the Mid-Atlantic All-Hazards Consortium, who saw value in the effort and provided much support. And last, but certainly not least, a special tribute to the fine men and women of the New Jersey Office of Homeland Security and Preparedness, the U.S. Department of Homeland Security, and all my HSA colleagues who continue to serve unselfishly.

RLC

References

The McGraw-Hill Homeland Security Handbook, David Kamien, 2006, The McGraw-Hill Company, Inc.

New World Coming: American Security in the 21st Century, USCNS/21, Washington, DC: US Government Printing Office, September 1999), v.

Quadrennial Homeland Security Review Report: A Strategic Framework for a Secure Homeland, February 2010, Department of Homeland Security printing. Also, *see www.dhs.gov.*

Homeland Security Presidential Directive #5 (HSPD-5), President George W. Bush, E.O. 26, 1996, and updated 2006 as Executive Order 26.1

The National Commission on Terrorist Attacks Upon the United States, aka, The 9/11 Commission Report, May 27, 2004

2009 National Infrastructure Protection Plan—Partnering to Enhance Protection and Resiliency Department of Homeland Security—2009

Society of Actuaries, Casualty Actuarial Society website, www. beanactuary.com

Fusion Center Guidelines—Developing and Sharing Information and Intelligence in a New Era, August 2006, U.S. Department of Homeland Security, U.S. Department of Justice

FY-10 Guidelines for Emergency Operations Center Grants Program, FEMA, Department of Homeland Security FY-10 Budget.

The Robert T. Stafford Disaster Relief and Emergency Assistance Act (Stafford Act), Pub. L. 100-707, 1988 amended version of the Disaster Relief Act of 1974, Pub. L. 93-288.

The Essentials of Terror Medicine, Shmuel C. Shapira, Leonard Cole, Jeffery S. Hammond, September 2009, Springer Publishing

Homeland Security Presidential Directive HSPD-7, Critical Infrastructure Identification, Prioritization, and Protection, December 17, 2003, President George W. Bush

Directive EU COM 786, European Commission, (2006)

Critical Thinking: Moving from Infrastructure Protection to Infrastructure Resilience, George Mason University, School of Law, Critical Infrastructure Protection Program, Discussion Studies Series, February 2007

The Edge of Disaster: Rebuilding a Resilient Nation, Flynn, Stephen E., Random House Inc., New York, 2007.

Bioterrorim Overview, Centers for Disease Control and Prevention, 2008-02-12, retrieved 2009-05-22.

Disaster Response: Principles of Preparation and Coordination, adapted from Auf derHeide. 1989. St. Louis, Missouri: C.V. Mosby and Company, pp. 14-17.

Obama looking to give new life to Immigration Reform, March 4, 2010, Los Angeles Times, Peter Nicholas.

Is the United States Safer from a Terrorist Attack Today than before Sept.11?, An interview with Michael Chertoff and Gus Coldebella, New Jersey Lawyer Magazine, October 2007, No. 248

International Ship and Port Facility Security Code, amendment to the Safety of Life at Sea (SOLAS) Convention (1974/1988), London July 1, 2004

Forging America's New Normalcy:Securing Our Homeland, Preserving Our Liberty, December 15, 2003,The Fifth Annual Report to the President and the Congress, Retrieved from http://www.rand.org/nsrd/terrpanel

Infrastructure Report Card, American Society of Civil Engineers, ASCE (May 2009)

Winning the Long War, Carafano, James J. and Rosenweig, Paul (2005), Heritage Books, Washington, DC

American Jihad, Emerson, Steven (2002), FreePress Paperbacks, New York, NY

War Footing, Gaffney, Frank J. (2006) Naval Institute Press, Annapolis, MD

The Birth of NFPA, Grant, Casey Cavanaugh PE. (1996), NFPA Journal®, Retrieved from http://www.nfpa.org/item

NFPA/Overview/History, Mayer, Matt A. (2009), "An Analysis of Federal, State, and Local Homeland Security Budgets", Heritage Foundation, Center for Data Analysis, Washington, DC

NACo Policy Agenda for Disaster Preparedness, Mitigation, Response and Recovery, National Association of Counties. Retrieved from http://www.naco.org/

Overview of States Homeland Security Governance, National Governor's Association, Center for Best Practices. Retrieved from http://www.nga.org/Files/pdf/HOMESECSTRUCTURES.pdf

A Governor's Guide to Homeland Security Center for Best Practices, National Governor's Association, 03/14/2007, Homeland Security & Technology Division Publications. Retrieved from http://www.nga.org/Files/pdf/0703GOVGUIDEHS.PDF

National Emergency Management Association National Homeland Security Consortium, Retrieved from http://www.nemaweb.org/?2091

Emergency Management: The American Experience 1900-2005, Rubin, Claire R., Editor., Second Edition (Fairfax, VA: PERI, 2007)

Schneier, Bruce (2003), "Beyond Fear", Copernicus Books, New York, NY

Unfinished Business at FEMA-A National Preparedness Perspective, Schrader, Dennis R., May 14, 2009, The Heritage Foundation, Retrieved from http://www.heritage.org/press/events/ev051409a.cfm

Acts of God, Steinberg, Ted. (2000), Oxford University Press, New York, NY, U.S. Chamber of Commerce-Business Civic Leadership Center (June 2009). A Critical

Role-Top Ten Policies that States Need to Recover from Disaster,

Index

About the Author

Richard "Dick" Cañas is the former Director of the New Jersey Office of Homeland Security and Preparedness (2006-2010), and a member of the U. S. Department of Homeland Security's Homeland Security Advisory Council (HSAC) (2009-Present). Prior to joining OHSP, he managed information-sharing programs for the U. S. National Guard Bureau and the U. S. National Security Agency.

In 1998 Cañas concluded a 26 year career with the U. S. Department of Justice, which included serving as Director of the National Drug Intelligence Center, Special Agent-in-Charge of the Phoenix Office of the Drug Enforcement Administration, Special Advisor to the Central Intelligence Agency, and Director at the White House's National Security Council and various domestic and international assignments while with DEA. He served four years at the NSC as Director for counterterrorism and counternarcotics under both President George H.W. Bush and President William J. Clinton.

Cañas has a diverse background in state and federal law enforcement, both domestic and foreign. Before starting his 24 years with DEA, he was a police officer and detective for the Salinas, California Police Department for eight years.

A native Californian, he is a graduate of San Jose State University, and has a Life-time Police Science Teaching Credential from the University of California at Berkeley. He has taught criminal justice subjects in California, Virginia and Tennessee and authored numerous articles on a variety of national security, intelligence, and homeland security subjects. He has also authored two historical novels about El Salvador, *Jaguars* and *Decade of Iron*.

He is currently a resident of Brentwood, Tennessee and continues to consult for the public and private sector on homeland and national security matters and serves on various national, state, and university boards.